Billboards

*The Secrets of
Free Money for Doing Nothing
and the Coming
Landowner Revolution*

by
Jeffrey Thomas

Copyright© 2001 by National Landowner Network, LLC.

All rights reserved.
No part of this book may be reproduced, stored in a retrieval system, or transmitted by any means, electronic, mechanical, photocopying, recording, or otherwise, without written permission from the author.

ISBN: 0-75962-973-0

This book is printed on acid free paper.

1stbooks rev. 8/16/01

*To anyone who has ever
stood up to a bully.*

The Universe is change; our life is what our thoughts make it.

>Marcus Aurelius Antonius
>A.D. 121 – 180

Read this first

My wife and I once hosted a party, and several of the guests played table tennis, also known as Ping-Pong (although the friendly Ping-Pong people will thank you if you recognize their protected brand name). Anyway, one of the guests was being a jerk by destroying everyone he played. Like most insecure people, he had no grace whatsoever. The more lopsided the score, the more he strutted. And the more he strutted, the more he disrupted the friendly tone of the party. Finally, no one would play him. Then he looked at me with his beady rodentious eyes. "Well?" he said. I turned to my wife. She sighed. "Keep it nice," she said. "We're the hosts."

After a short warm up, I bopped over a bunny serve to start the game. Nothing threatening or aggressive. Just a polite, innocent tap. And he absolutely crushed it. Before I even moved my paddle, the ball screamed over the net, scored a point, and smacked me in the stomach so hard I could feel the little red sting under my shirt. Like a cocky boxer, the other guy then juked back and forth on the balls of his feet. "I won my college championship four years in a row," he said with a smirk. "Never lost a game." The other guests gathered to watch the slaughter.

Later, one person told me that from the look on my face, it appeared I was going to quit. No. I knew the other guy had gone to a dinky little school that no one had ever heard of, and had fattened his ego on hapless dupes. I, on the other hand, had lost literally thousands of Ping-Pong games over the years. Jeepers, I lost all the time. But I always played top competition, and whatever skill I had came from continually getting creamed by superior, often national-level, players. I took a deep breath, and again looked toward my wife. Our eyes met. She knew. "Fine," she said. "Go ahead."

I beat him 21-1.

The significance of this story, if any, I leave to the reader.

* * *

This book presents new business models for the multi-billion dollar outdoor advertising industry. To enhance speed and understanding, the material is a simple conversation between a Good Samaritan named, conveniently, Good Sam, and a man who has a billboard on his own (not Good Sam's) land. His name, also convenient, is Landowner. Alert readers will notice their fictional conversation includes overt references to this book, even though their conversation is this book. A time puzzle to be sure, but necessary.

The most important background you need is that Landowner, like hundreds of thousands of other landowners across the country, allowed a billboard company to temporarily erect a billboard on his land in exchange for a fee. Landowner owns the land, the billboard company owns the billboard, and the sign stays up (and the advertising money comes in) only as long as the lease is in effect. That arrangement is the foundation of outdoor advertising, and no one has ever questioned it.

Until now.

Unfortunately, our Landowner signed his lease with limited information regarding gross revenues or profit margins. In fact, he put little thought into the decision at all. The billboard company made an offer, and Landowner blindly accepted it. Landowner wasn't aware of other options because he operated from a position of weakness. He was alone. He had no allies. He had nowhere to go for help. With this book, that will change. If you are one of the approximately 800,000 billboard landowners in the United States, this is terrific news. Conversely, individuals aligned with the old billboard enterprises may be somewhat less enthusiastic.

You should also know that this book does not necessarily portray all billboard companies or billboard people. Any assumption to the contrary is wrong. Further, no cities, states, companies, or individuals are identified by name, which means only the guilty will recognize themselves and be offended.

If this were a movie instead of a book, it might begin as these words scrolled across the screen:

> "All names and locations were omitted to prevent misguided lawyers from harassing the author with frivolous and vexatious lawsuits initiated by rich spoiled crybabies."

Now let's join Good Sam and Landowner, and see what they have to say.

Chapter 2

GOOD SAM

I understand you own some land that has a billboard on it.

LANDOWNER

Yes, I do. That was explained in this book's terrific introduction. Did you notice the author's command of language? His error-free style is the most unique I've ever read.

GOOD SAM

But you don't own the billboard?

LANDOWNER

No. As was also explained this book's truly stellar introduction, a billboard company owns it. They just pay me to keep it there. Besides, when the billboard guy first approached me years ago, I asked if I could put up my own sign instead of his. I wasn't serious about it, just curious.

GOOD SAM

What did he say?

LANDOWNER

He said only federally licensed billboard companies could own and run the signs. Otherwise, he said, we'd have billboards everywhere. So I took the easy money, and never gave it a second thought.

GOOD SAM

That means you don't know anything at all about the billboard business? You don't know about revenue or profit margins?

LANDOWNER

No. Should I?

GOOD SAM

Yes, because then you could make an informed decision about why you're allowing a billboard company to make all the big money while you get hardly any.

LANDOWNER

But what about federal licenses and all that?

$2,000/mo per side

GOOD SAM

It was gibberish meant to steer you away from a line of thought detrimental to his industry. The last thing in the world he wanted you to think about was ownership of your own billboard.

LANDOWNER

What other options do I have?

GOOD SAM

You have at least two. How much more money you might make will depend on things like the size and location of your billboard, and also the unit's traffic count and client demand. But with one of the options, you might increase your money tenfold.

LANDOWNER

Tenfold! Wow. Can you give me some numbers?

GOOD SAM

Sure. Let's use you as an example. What's the advertising rate for the sign that's on your land?

LANDOWNER

A friend told me the billboard company gets $2,000 a month per side, for a total of $4,000 a month.

GOOD SAM

That means it's probably a 14 foot by 48 foot billboard called a bulletin.

Bulletin

[Handwritten at top: 14x48' Bulletin, 12x24 poster, <700 ¢p/side]

[Handwritten in margin: posters]

LANDOWNER

Are there different sized billboards?

GOOD SAM

Yes, for the purposes of our conversation, there are two main sizes. In addition to the 14 by 48 foot bulletins, there are also 12 by 24 foot poster units. There are other sizes, too, both bigger and smaller, but bulletins and posters are the majority.

LANDOWNER

Bulletins and posters. That's easy enough. Is the $4,000 per month an average rate for bulletins?

GOOD SAM

There's really no such thing as an average rate. Some 14 by 48 footers might rent to an advertising client for only $400 a month. In a different market, others can rent for over $10,000 a month. And although it goes against logic, rates are not dictated solely by traffic count.

LANDOWNER

So there's a spread in rates, even for the same sized signs.

GOOD SAM

Yes. In your case, though, the billboard company gets $48,000 a year in space revenue.

LANDOWNER

Space revenue?

[Handwritten margin note: PROFIT MARGIN 50%+]

GOOD SAM

That's the money from renting out the advertising space. There is also production revenue, which can be thousands of dollars.

LANDOWNER

I see. But that's gross income.

GOOD SAM

It certainly is.

LANDOWNER

You know what I mean. What's the profit margin?

GOOD SAM

Overall, possibly around 50 percent. Maybe more, maybe less. It depends on the company. It could even top 70 percent. But for our discussion, 50 percent is a good amount to start with until someone proves otherwise by opening their financial books for review.

LANDOWNER

Opening their books?

GOOD SAM

Yes. If any billboard company tries to get you to do anything regarding your lease, your first and only response is to demand open financials. Not just selected printouts, either. Everything. And get them for the past five years, just to be safe. Otherwise, don't even listen to them. No open books, no conversations about the lease.

LANDOWNER

Some billboard companies aren't going to like that.

GOOD SAM

Tough. By the time we're done talking, there will be a lot of things they don't like.

Chapter 3

LANDOWNER

After hearing those numbers, I feel sort of silly for agreeing to the original lease.

GOOD SAM

Why?

LANDOWNER

Because the billboard guy was so convincing. He said my money was guaranteed, even if the billboard company had no income from the site. He made it sound like they were taking a big risk, while I was getting free money for doing nothing.

GOOD SAM

Free money for doing nothing. That sure sounds nice, doesn't it? But what he didn't tell you is that most billboards have nearly 100 percent annual occupancy rates, so there was virtually no risk on his part.

LANDOWNER

Still, I'm finding it hard to accept that he got the better of me in a business deal. He seemed so unsophisticated.

GOOD SAM

You shouldn't feel bad. It was probably just an act on his part.

LANDOWNER

How so?

GOOD SAM

One billboard guy described it as camouflage. His strategy was to wear blue jeans instead of a suit when talking to a landowner. Then, in an aw-shucks voice, he described the billboard business. "We get up every day at five in the morning," he said. "We work heavy equipment until we can barely move our arms, and if we're lucky we might have a buck or two to show for it at the end of the week. Then Monday rolls around and we start the whole thing over again."

LANDOWNER

Like he was a real workin' man. But I fell for it.

GOOD SAM

That's because it's a very effective technique. The billboard guy knew if he wore a nice suit and met you in an expensive office, you'd smell money and raise the price of the lease. He also knew that if the billboard business sounded brutal, his offer to you would seem even better. And by the way, billboard companies don't use the term "landowners" to describe people like you.

LANDOWNER

What do they call us?

GOOD SAM

Lessors.

LANDOWNER

Lessers? Meaning they don't think we're as good as they are, and that they are somehow superior to us?

GOOD SAM

No, *lessors*. Although your definition might still apply.

LANDOWNER

Let's use your term. Landowners. It shows more respect. But no matter what you call me, it's embarrassing that I was fooled so easily, and that I settled for so little, when so much money was available.

GOOD SAM

Yet you're very typical. Some billboard companies just mail out lease renewals informing the landowners, without discussion, of the new rates. And many landowners meekly accept that number. Sometimes the rate even goes down, and the landowners accept it. But since you brought it up, let's look at your numbers. Of the $48,000 annual space revenue, how much does the billboard company pay you for your site lease?

LANDOWNER

Uh, $175 a month.

GOOD SAM

Per side, or total?

LANDOWNER

Total.

GOOD SAM

How did you arrive at that number? Was it based on a percentage of revenue?

LANDOWNER

No. It wasn't based on anything at all. I guess we just sort of made it up, although he did say it was the standard industry rate.

GOOD SAM

The standard industry rate?

LEASE PMNTS
5% - 10%

LANDOWNER

Yeah. That sounded real official then. But now that I think about it, it sounds sort of dorky.

GOOD SAM

So $175 a month is $2,100 per year, or less than 4.4 percent of the $48,000 in space revenue that the billboard company gets.

LANDOWNER

It's even worse that you thought, huh?

GOOD SAM

No. A lot of billboard companies try to keep their overall lease payments to around five or ten percent.

LEASE PMNTS 5% - 10%

Chapter 4

GOOD SAM

Who pays the utilities for your billboard?

LANDOWNER

Utilities?

GOOD SAM

The billboard has lights at night, right? Who pays the electric bill, you or the billboard company?

LANDOWNER

Why, they do, I think. Don't they?

GOOD SAM

Not always. I heard of one landowner who was paid $100 a month for the billboard lease, but unknown to him the electricity was tapped into his line instead of being hooked up to an independent meter.

LANDOWNER

How much did his utility bill increase?

GOOD SAM

It went up by an extra $120 a month.

LANDOWNER

So he was actually losing $20 a month. Didn't anyone notice?

GOOD SAM

It was a business line, not residential, so the utility bills weren't monitored closely.

LANDOWNER

I bet the billboard people got a big laugh out of that.

GOOD SAM

Oh, they thought it was hilarious. The same billboard company also had some dormant no-pay leases, which meant they kept revenue-producing billboards on land without compensating the landowners at all.

LANDOWNER

No compensation at all? That sounds odd. Could the billboard company have found those landowners if they had tried?

GOOD SAM

Sure. In many cases, they had the addresses and telephone numbers.

LANDOWNER

But they didn't try? Not even a couple of phone calls to get things square again?

GOOD SAM

Correct. The dormant leases were ones that, for various reasons, had fallen through the cracks. Since the landowners didn't protect their own interests, the billboard company saw no reason to do it for them.

LANDOWNER

But that goes beyond aggressive business. It's more like finding someone's wallet, and not returning it even though it has identification. If it's not technically stealing, it's as close as you can get.

GOOD SAM

That's one way to look at it.

LANDOWNER

Well, I think it's the only way. Are all billboard companies like that?

GOOD SAM

Hey, I'm not trying to give you the impression that all billboard companies or billboard people are dishonest. I'm sure there are many fine people in the industry. But when it comes to leases, it is you against them, and trusting the wrong person could be a big mistake.

LANDOWNER

Even if he's a golfing buddy?

GOOD SAM

It depends on how expensive you want your golf to be. I heard of one major billboard company that gave bonuses to managers who reduced lease payments to landowners, even though the billboard company was knocking down profit margins of 50 percent.

LANDOWNER

How were the bonuses calculated?

GOOD SAM

The managers got a percentage of the lease reduction.

LANDOWNER

So the less money the landowner made, the more money the manager put in his pocket. That means a manager's financial interests were directly opposed to those of a landowner.

GOOD SAM

Exactly. The billboard company even created a newsletter so all their managers across the country could compare notes on how to pay less money for the leases.

LANDOWNER

It sounds like I should have based my lease on a percentage of revenue, instead of a fixed amount. That way, I'd make more money as the billboard company made more money.

GOOD SAM

Even that may not have protected you. I heard of one landowner who did, and still lost out.

LANDOWNER

How?

GOOD SAM

The billboard company agreed to pay him 20 percent of the sign's revenue, and showed him the current rate card to establish the base amount. Let's say the listed rate was around $2,000 per month. But the billboard actually sold for an off-card rate of over $5,000 per month, and the $2,000 figure was meaningless. So instead of 20 percent of the revenue, he actually got only eight percent. And he still didn't get any production money.

LANDOWNER

That means the billboard people lied to the landowner, and cheated him, all because he didn't know any better.

GOOD SAM

That's one way to put it.

production revenue

Chapter 5

LANDOWNER

You mentioned production revenue. What is that?

GOOD SAM

It's money that comes from painting or printing the billboard's design. It also comes from general labor and construction. Production fees generate tremendous profits, often for very little work.

LANDOWNER

How?

GOOD SAM

Let's use poster billboards as an example.

LANDOWNER

The ones with paper pasted on them?

GOOD SAM

Exactly. The ad designs go up just like wallpaper. Large national clients usually provide their own paper. For local clients, the billboard company often orders the posters for them by working with a printing company.

LANDOWNER

That's a nice thing to do.

GOOD SAM

Maybe, except some billboard companies double or triple the cost before billing the clients. Some billboard companies even own their own printing companies, and make money on both ends of the transaction without the clients knowing about it.

LANDOWNER

What do posters cost?

GOOD SAM

It varies, depending on the complexity of the poster, as well as the quantity ordered. Not including the monthly space rental rate, posters could be $50 each, or $500 each. But let's say there are 30 posters ordered at $100 each, for $3,000. If that amount is doubled or tripled, it means the client actually pays $6,000 or $9,000 in production costs.

EXTENSIONS
$30/SQ FT.

LANDOWNER

What does the billboard company do to earn that money?

GOOD SAM

A few minutes of paperwork. And almost never do the landowners share in the production revenue. The billboard company keeps it all.

LANDOWNER

Amazing. Are there any other examples?

GOOD SAM

Sure. Have you seen how some of the large 14 x 48 foot billboards have parts of the design that go outside the frame?

LANDOWNER

Yeah. They sometimes make the design look sort of three-dimensional.

GOOD SAM

Right. Those add-ons are called extensions. They're often made out of scrap plywood, and are simply bolted onto the frame.

LANDOWNER

How much does the client pay for extensions?

GOOD SAM

All companies are different, but some charge around $30 a square foot or more.

23

[handwritten margin note: 70 SQ.FT. EXTENSIONS ALLOWED BY ZONING (MAX)]

LANDOWNER

How many square feet are there in an extension?

GOOD SAM

About 70 feet are often allowed by zoning, but it varies from town to town.

LANDOWNER

That means the billboard company gets $2,100 for scrap plywood that's worth maybe - what? A hundred bucks?

GOOD SAM

Not even that, because the plywood is used over and over for different clients. In fact, whenever one billboard accountant used to get a work order for production, she would cackle and say "Boy, we make out like bandits on this stuff."

LANDOWNER

She cackled? Isn't that something witches do?

GOOD SAM

Yes.

LANDOWNER

Of course, if a bandit is defined as someone who steals for a living, some might say she had a valid point.

Chapter 6

LANDOWNER

I had no idea billboards were so profitable.

GOOD SAM

Well, every company is different. But once, a smug billboard company owner gave an interview. He talked about how billboard companies don't have news teams to pay, like television and radio stations do. And how billboard companies don't have stories to print, the way newspapers and magazines do. Then he smiled and said "But we surely do enjoy raising our rates."

LANDOWNER

He said that? What a dope.

GOOD SAM

Another manager said the billboard business was an industry with good years, great years, and I-can't-believe-we-get-away-with-this years. Finally, yet another manager figured out he could close his branch for an entire year and still make a substantial profit.

LANDOWNER

How?

GOOD SAM

Just by letting the existing clients continue up on the billboards. He could literally lock the office doors and turn out the lights, as long as someone took the checks to the bank every month. And it's not just the signs that are valuable. The leases themselves are solid gold.

LANDOWNER

You mean once a billboard goes up.

GOOD SAM

No, I mean just the leases, with no billboards.

LANDOWNER

I'm not following you.

GOOD SAM

I've heard of people who became rich without ever erecting a single billboard, and without owning any land.

selling leases

LANDOWNER

How?

GOOD SAM

They would canvass a city for billboard sites, then sign as many landowners as possible to contracts. Then they would sell their signed leases to an existing billboard company.

LANDOWNER

They would sell just the leases? For how much?

GOOD SAM

It varied around the country, but a couple of dozen good locations in the right city might sell for over a million dollars.

LANDOWNER

Okay, I'm going to rephrase this to make sure I understand. A guy got some leases signed. Just pieces of paper. He didn't buy the land, or have an option to buy the land, or anything like that. In fact, he didn't have much cash outlay at all.

GOOD SAM

Correct.

LANDOWNER

And there weren't any actual billboards erected yet. No advertising clients, no designs, nothing else. Right?

GOOD SAM

Right. Erecting the billboards was the easy part. Finding advertising clients was easy, too. The hard part was finding legal building sites, and that's what the person sold.

LANDOWNER

Just the leases themselves.

GOOD SAM

I think we've made that point.

LANDOWNER

I know, but it just seems so unbelievable. Why in the world would just leases be worth so much money?

GOOD SAM

You tell me.

LANDOWNER

I don't know anything about the billboard business. I can't figure out that sort of thing.

GOOD SAM

Yes, you can. We've only talked for a few minutes, and you already know enough to answer your own question. So walk me through the numbers on 24 prime locations, and tell me why they're worth a million dollars.

LANDOWNER

Well, okay. I'll try. First, we have 24 locations. And let's say they're all double-sided, which gives us 48 faces. How much do they sell for?

GOOD SAM

It depends on things like the city, the traffic count, and the competition. But go ahead and use the same $2,000 we talked about earlier.

LANDOWNER

Okay. That gives us $2,000 per month per face. And we have 48 faces. How much is that?

GOOD SAM

$96,000 per month, or $1,152,000 per year.

LANDOWNER

What's the profit margin?

GOOD SAM

Let's say 50 percent.

LANDOWNER

How much do the structures themselves cost?

[Handwritten margin note: COST TO BUILD A BILLBOARD $5-$50K. CAN DEPRECIATE OVER TIME.]

GOOD SAM

It varies a lot. There are different kinds of signs, and many billboard companies do some or all of the work themselves. If a landowner hired an independent construction company and paid full price, it could range from $5,000 to $50,000, depending on the unit.

LANDOWNER

But even at the high end of those rates, the initial cost pays for itself pretty quickly.

GOOD SAM

Actually, you'd probably depreciate the cost over time. But either way, because you get to increase your ad rates, you'll eventually make a profit of over a million dollars a year.

LANDOWNER

So that's why a billboard company would pay a million dollars just for leases.

GOOD SAM

Yes. Another reason is because an existing billboard company will do almost anything to gain the double advantage of increasing its own inventory while preventing competition from gaining a foothold in the market.

LANDOWNER

Billboard companies don't like competition?

GOOD SAM

They're terrified of it. Some billboard companies even refuse to operate in a market unless they have a monopoly or near-monopoly situation.

Chapter 7

LANDOWNER

You mentioned two primary options for a landowner. What are they?

GOOD SAM

Before I answer that, you need to listen very carefully, because this next sentence is perhaps the most important one of our entire conversation. It is very, very serious.

LANDOWNER

I understand. Go ahead.

GOOD SAM

Peppy preppies pack perky purple parkas.

[Handwritten note: LEASE = % OF AUDITED REVENUE PLUS PRODUCTION]

LANDOWNER

Huh?

GOOD SAM

Sorry, I was just trying to relieve the tension. Okay, here's the important sentence. Regardless of which option is selected, ALL the landowners in the various markets must work together and deal with billboard companies from a position of united strength, instead of as scattered individuals who may be manipulated or intimidated.

LANDOWNER

That's a long sentence. Perhaps you should repeat it.

GOOD SAM

Join forces or be bugs on a windshield.

LANDOWNER

Got it. What's the first option?

GOOD SAM

The first option is the obvious one. Using the leverage of legally cancelling or not renewing their incredibly valuable leases, the united landowners will negotiate for substantially higher lease payments. Unlike most current leases, however, the payments will be based on a percentage of audited revenue, including production.

LANDOWNER

Why should the revenue be audited?

GOOD SAM

Because with creative accounting, some companies hide numbers the way squirrels hide nuts.

LANDOWNER

And in this case, it would be our nuts we were protecting. What kind of increase could we expect?

GOOD SAM

It would depend on the situation, but you could probably triple your lease payments with hardly any effort at all, and the billboard company would still be profitable. But even that may be settling for too little.

LANDOWNER

And settling for too little is something we've done for too long. But I'll repeat what I said earlier. Some billboard companies won't like any of this. They're used to us being submissive, and this new attitude will be a shock.

GOOD SAM

I agree, and I think that's the weakness of a forced relationship between united landowners and the old billboard companies. My guess is that billboard company owners who are used to 50 or 60 percent profit margins are not going to suddenly take 10 or 20 percent margins. Their egos just won't let them.

LANDOWNER

What if they open their books and show us there isn't more money to give?

GOOD SAM

Then I would question their ability to effectively run a billboard company, and the landowners should find someone else who would better maximize landowner value. In either case, highly profitable or not, my guess is that once the billboard company owners got over being angry, some of them would discuss the second option for the landowners.

LANDOWNER

Which is?

GOOD SAM

A complete buyout of the old billboard company, giving total ownership and control to the landowners. Assets would include buildings, equipment, personnel, client records, and of course the signs themselves.

LANDOWNER

A complete buyout? Wow, that sounds cool.

GOOD SAM

And if a billboard company has branches in, say, five or 25 or 50 different markets, the landowners from all those markets should work together for a multi-market buyout. It should not be done one market at a time. That is very important.

LANDOWNER

How will we know if there are other markets?

GOOD SAM

Check the media kits and Web sites of the billboard company in question, or use the Internet and look under the national Yellow Pages. Remember, the landowners in those other markets are your allies, even though you've never met them. Their success is your success. The more you communicate with them, the better.

LANDOWNER

How much does a typical billboard company cost?

GOOD SAM

It depends, and besides, what billboard companies have cost and what they will cost are two different things. In the past, some valuations were based on profit multiples. Others were based on revenue multiples. Some focused on projected earnings, others on trailing earnings. And all the valuations varied from year to year, depending on market conditions.

LANDOWNER

But now that will change? How?

GOOD SAM

Let's say a hypothetical multi-market billboard company grosses $100 million annually at a 50 percent profit margin, and has a market valuation of ten times revenue, or $1 billion. Are you with me so far?

LANDOWNER

Yes. And I understand this is just an example. An actual market valuation might not be ten times revenue. It could be more or less.

GOOD SAM

Correct. But in this case, there's a billboard company supposedly worth $1 billion that the landowners want to buy. But that $1 billion valuation was before the landowners organized. After the landowners get together, the historical valuations cease to exist, and the landowners will likely be able to buy the billboard company for a whole lot less than what it had been worth.

LANDOWNER

How much less? After all, the old owner will be pretty snippy about this.

GOOD SAM

Here's how it might play out. On one hand, the landowners will not want the expense of having to recreate the entire industry infrastructure. On the other hand, faced with 100 percent cancellations or non-renewals from the united landowners, regardless of when those changes become effective, the old billboard people are toast.

LANDOWNER

The takedown costs alone would be extraordinary. They'd be in the scrap metal business, not the billboard business.

GOOD SAM

Right. And somewhere between those two extremes is a buyout price the old billboard people should grudgingly accept once they start making decisions based on logic instead of emotion. It will take them a while to reach that perspective, though. There will be more than a few tantrums along the way from people who are decidedly unused to being challenged.

LANDOWNER

Then give me a number. In this example, how much would it cost the landowners to buy the billboard company that grosses $100 million a year at a 50 percent profit margin?

GOOD SAM

My guess is no more than one times annual revenue, or $100 million. And I say that not as a starting point in negotiations, but as the final, agreed-upon offer.

Chapter 8

LANDOWNER

If we're going to buy a billboard company, we'll need money. Where will it come from? Venture capitalists?

GOOD SAM

In the start-up phase, some venture capital money will be necessary. But not for the whole takeover.

LANDOWNER

Will venture capitalists be interested in working with us?

GOOD SAM

Interested? There will be brawls in the hallway as they fight to be first in line.

LANDOWNER

Do you really think so?

GOOD SAM

If the money people have any sense, yes, because the quality of investment we're discussing is extraordinary. Think about it. There are existing customers. High demand. High advertiser renewal rates. Decades of industry growth and performance. Prohibitive barriers to entry for competitors. Most importantly, there are profits, and profits, and profits.

LANDOWNER

Are all those things important?

GOOD SAM

For anyone worth talking to, yes. There are even clearly defined exit strategies. For investors, it just doesn't get any better than that.

LANDOWNER

But I thought venture capitalists preferred faddish, high-risk, incomprehensible start-ups that are doomed to failure. We, on the other hand, will be just the opposite of all that. Won't that work against us?

GOOD SAM

I believe there will be at least a few intelligent groups interested in helping a landowner-controlled billboard industry, despite the fact that the business model is simple and easy to understand.

LANDOWNER

Won't we seem boring compared to sexy technology companies?

GOOD SAM

If you're talking to someone competent, profits are never boring. Besides, I think you'll only need venture capital for the early stages. For the purchase itself, straight financing should be readily available, provided you have a strong management team to run the company.

LANDOWNER

Are you saying we can just go out and get a $100 million loan?

GOOD SAM

Sure. Or even better, you can pay the former owner over time, and let the cash flow of the new company service the debt.

LANDOWNER

Wait a minute. The old owner's former employees would provide the cash flow from his former billboards, and we would use that money to pay him for what used to be his own company, all at ten cents on the dollar? That would be very funny.

GOOD SAM

I'm not saying every deal will turn out that way. But I believe the general concepts are sound, even though the final numbers and percentages could change. On the other hand, the example might be quite accurate. Once the owner stops whooping around like an irate chimp, he might realize that a $100 million is still a lot of money. It just isn't $1 billion.

LANDOWNER

So regardless of which option we choose, the two key elements are a united and organized group of landowners, and a strong management team. Correct?

GOOD SAM

Yes. If you organize and work together, the financial gains may be more than you ever imagined.

LANDOWNER

Because, in our example, we'd own a company worth $100 million.

GOOD SAM

One hundred million? Gosh, I'm sorry, I guess I didn't make that clear. Once you own the company, you should set about to restore the market value back to the original $1 billion.

LANDOWNER

Can we do that?

GOOD SAM

I think so, yes.

LANDOWNER

So we'd find a company worth $1 billion, pay $100 million for it, then after we bought it, we'd make it worth $1 billion again?

GOOD SAM

Yep.

LANDOWNER

Wow. What would the venture capitalists want in return for their early money?

GOOD SAM

I don't know. I've never worked with venture capitalists.

LANDOWNER

But if you had to guess, how would you work with them?

GOOD SAM

I'd just sit down with them and in plain English explain the needs and expectations of the landowners. Then I would listen carefully to the needs and expectations of the venture capitalists. Once risk was assessed, we could identify an aligned deal that was in the best interests of both sides. Maybe I'm naive, but that's how I'd do it.

Chapter 9

LANDOWNER

What if neither option works? What if the billboard people refuse to pay us more money, but we can't buy them out either? What then?

GOOD SAM

Then the landowners, as a group, will legally cancel or not renew their leases, and all the billboards will come down. The landowners will lose their lease payments, and the billboard company will go out of business.

LANDOWNER

That's what it will come down to, isn't it?

GOOD SAM

Yes. And if it comes to that point, what do you think will happen?

LANDOWNER

My guess is the billboard people will revisit the first two options, and we'll work out some sort of a deal. Probably a total buyout. Just like you said.

GOOD SAM

Sure. The billboard people can have part of something, or all of nothing. It's their choice.

LANDOWNER

But the billboard companies are big and rich. Maybe it would be safer if we remain passive and docile, and just hope for the best.

GOOD SAM

Stop thinking like that. Those days are over. As long as you work together, you landowners have a tremendous amount of leverage. I'm not saying you should turn into arrogant jerks, but you will become a force. You will have power. You will not be ignored.

LANDOWNER

You sound so confident.

GOOD SAM

So should you. Yes, there will be problems. Yes, there will be obstacles. And you may have to compromise along the way. But a united group of billboard landowners is a colossal organization. You need to recognize that, and adjust your thinking accordingly.

Chapter 10

LANDOWNER

When a billboard company hears that the landowners are going to organize and work together, can't the owner just cash out and run?

GOOD SAM

No, because the billboard company will be worthless to anyone other than the landowners. There simply won't be any other buyers.

LANDOWNER

Can you be more specific as to why that's the case?

GOOD SAM

Billboard company valuations depend on the assumed renewals of landowner leases. Without those guaranteed renewals, there is no resale value. And the fact that billboard companies are so expensive is exactly why no one will buy them once the possibility of organized landowners becomes known.

LANDOWNER

If we're the only buyers, why should we pay even $100 million for our hypothetical company?

GOOD SAM

That's a good point. When you look at it that way, I suppose some people might think the landowners were being generous if they took the company off the previous owner's hands for free.

LANDOWNER

But this is all based on the assumed collapse of corporate valuations, and that's just theory, right?

GOOD SAM

No, and this little story proves it. One time a guy called a billboard company that was selling a handful of sites for several hundred thousand dollars.

LANDOWNER

The company owned just the billboards, but not the land?

GOOD SAM

Right. And the potential buyer asked about the leases. He was told they were secure.

LANDOWNER

What did that mean?

GOOD SAM

That the lessors would continue to act like sheep and renew their leases for pennies on the dollar. Then the buyer said he wanted protection in case any of the landowners didn't renew their leases.

LANDOWNER

What did the billboard person say to that?

GOOD SAM

He said the assumption of lease renewals would be written into the contract because, and I'm quoting here, "without the leases, there wasn't anything to sell."

LANDOWNER

He admitted that without the leases, the value of his billboard company was zero? That's amazing. And he wasn't selling guaranteed advertising contracts?

GOOD SAM

No. If the advertising clients cancelled, that was the new owner's problem.

LANDOWNER

So the only things he was selling were the leases, and the signs themselves. Were the signs new?

GOOD SAM

No. They looked at least 20 years old.

LANDOWNER

So the leases really are everything. And they're hard to replace?

GOOD SAM

Very hard. Impossible in many cases.

LANDOWNER

Then based on what we talked about earlier, that means leases without billboards are worth millions, but billboards without leases are worth nothing.

GOOD SAM

That's very well put.

LANDOWNER

And as a landowner, I control the lease.

GOOD SAM

True. And a large group of landowners controls a large group of leases. You just never knew it.

LANDOWNER

So what we're really saying here is that landowners have the legal right to either exercise existing cancellation clauses or not renew their leases with the old billboard company. And when the united landowners do that, the old billboard industry will crumble like a house of cards.

GOOD SAM

Yes. Providing they work together, the future of the entire United States outdoor advertising industry is in the hands of the landowners, not the current billboard companies.

Chapter 11

LANDOWNER

The landowners have to work together for anything to happen. I understand that. But how do we find each other?

GOOD SAM

Your first step is to call your local newspaper and try to get articles published as soon as possible. And maybe a review of this book, too.

LANDOWNER

Should the articles be about the landowners and their efforts to organize?

GOOD SAM

Yes. I think many editors will recognize the subject as a major national story with strong local ties.

LANDOWNER

Those local ties make it ideal for just about every newspaper in the country.

GOOD SAM

That's true. It impacts businesses, advertisers, and local governments in a significant way. If a newspaper has any concern at all for its community and readers, this story about billboard landowners will be of interest.

LANDOWNER

It would also be a great way for newspapers to show that their glory days as sources of news and breaking information haven't passed them by. How aggressive should we be with these calls?

GOOD SAM

Just be polite, because being pushy with a newspaper editor is like sticking your tongue out at a snapping turtle. It's quite counterproductive.

LANDOWNER

They're that tough?

GOOD SAM

They're beyond tough. If you want, just leave a message on their Voice Mail. That's not as good as a conversation, but it will still help.

LANDOWNER

Should we butter them up in the hope they'll be nice to us?

GOOD SAM

No. Editors are far too astute to fall for something that obvious. They're also hard-working and vastly underpaid for the valuable services they provide. It could even be argued that without our nation's network of superintelligent editors, democracy itself would be at risk.

LANDOWNER

Should we only call the newspapers in our own cities?

GOOD SAM

Call them first. But if you can spare an extra couple of minutes, try calling newspapers in nearby cities, too.

LANDOWNER

Is that all we have to do?

GOOD SAM

Call area bookstores to make sure they have this book in stock. Explain that the best newspapers with the smartest editors will soon be printing reviews, and that there are thousands of prime book buying landowners where you live.

LANDOWNER

Hang on, let me write that down. Call bookstore managers. Request they carry book. Mention smart newspaper editors who are immune to flattery. Okay, I got it. Anything else?

GOOD SAM

Tell them the book merits a feature display near the store's entrance. Something big that everyone will see as they walk in.

LANDOWNER

Ooh, good thinking. And maybe a colorful sign that asks "Do you have a billboard on your land?" How about that?

GOOD SAM

That's terrific. I wish I'd thought of it.

LANDOWNER

What about radio, or television, or magazines? Could they help us?

GOOD SAM

Hey, if you've got contacts with other print or broadcast media, go wild. It can only help.

Chapter 12

LANDOWNER

This will be a real grassroots campaign, won't it?

GOOD SAM

Yes, it will. But publicity and reviews alone won't be enough. You should also visit your city courthouse and obtain a government list of the landowners, including their names and mailing addresses.

LANDOWNER

A list of the landowners? Wow! How do we get one of those?

GOOD SAM

It's a little tricky, because you'll probably have to compile it yourself, and the process won't be the same for every city. First, go to the Planning Division, and explain that you're trying to find the names and addresses of all the area billboard landowners.

LANDOWNER

Names and addresses. Okay.

GOOD SAM

The person you're talking to probably won't understand, and will refer you to the billboard company or companies in your area, which is exactly what you don't want. So be persistent, but be polite, too.

LANDOWNER

Polite, because the city workers will be busy, and don't need some rude landowner disrupting their day.

GOOD SAM

Right. In fact, you should go in the morning, before everyone's day turns upside down. The odds are good that the city has some sort of billboard inventory list. Be prepared to pay a small fee for a copy of this list. Also, bring plenty of coins in case you need to photocopy anything.

LANDOWNER

Will that list have everything we need?

GOOD SAM

No, it's the first of two steps. The billboard inventory list will likely have the billboard site's parcel number, which will help you track down the landowner. Each site will have a different number.

Then you just visit the assessor's office to get your local land assessment records. Can you guess how these records are filed?

LANDOWNER

By parcel number?

GOOD SAM

Correct. The city assessor's office will either have a free Internet site where you can look up each landowner, or it will have public records which are available to you. If they're on a computer disc, you might have to buy or rent the assessor's records. Or they might be free. Again, be nice to anyone you talk to, and tell them what you're trying to do.

LANDOWNER

Ask for their help and advice.

GOOD SAM

Yes. Be patient, and eventually you'll get what you need. At the same time, remember this is all public record information you have a legal right to see.

LANDOWNER

Because someone somewhere has the information, right? Isn't it required for property taxes?

GOOD SAM

Yes. So be considerate and respectful, but don't allow someone to brush you off. Keep asking for supervisors if you have to, but don't leave until you either get what you came for or you get to the mayor.

LANDOWNER

Once I get all the parcel numbers from the billboard inventory list, do I just match those up with the assessor's records to get my list of landowners?

GOOD SAM

Yes. From there, you can mail letters and make phone calls to the people you need to reach. Remember that many landowners will be businesses, and that some landowners, particularly railroad companies, might have several billboards on their property. Maybe even dozens on a local level, or hundreds nationally. Such landowners should have top priority.

LANDOWNER

Contact the railroads first. Got it.

GOOD SAM

If you can't do the entire list, don't necessarily start at the front. Start at the end of the list, or the middle. That way, a greater number of landowners will be contacted, assuming that more than one person is doing the search.

LANDOWNER

Is there anything else we should do?

GOOD SAM

Remember that different towns and cities and counties will have systems unlike what we just discussed. So I tell you again, ask for help. Some of the records will even be written by hand, and not on computers at all. But if for some reason you can't get information from government records, you could always just go knock on the doors of the businesses and houses nearest to the billboards, concentrating on the busiest highways first. That would take some driving around, but it would get the job done.

LANDOWNER

Hey, I have an idea. Why not use the Internet?

GOOD SAM

How?

LANDOWNER

Each landowner could send 20 gazillion e-mails about this book to anyone and everyone he knew, with the hope that eventually, somehow, most of the landowners would be contacted. Maybe even 25 gazillion, just to be safe. We could send to individuals, but also places like financial sites, farming sites, and small business sites.

GOOD SAM

Great idea. But the message will have to be short and direct, while still communicating as much as possible.

LANDOWNER

Do you have something in mind?

GOOD SAM

An extension of your bookstore sign. Like this:

> Do you have a Billboard on your land? Do NOT sign a new lease with any billboard company until you meet with other area landowners to discuss what may be more profitable options. We need to work together! For more information, visit your Web site at www.unitedlandowners.com.

LANDOWNER

Wow, that gets right to the point. And our own little Web site, too. Will it be up and running right away?

GOOD SAM

It will exist, but the early stages won't be fancy, and you'll have to be patient as it evolves and grows as the landowners themselves evolve and grow. Eventually, though, it will be a terrific resource.

Chapter 13

LANDOWNER

I'm not sure how to say this, and I hope you don't get mad or anything, but this is starting to sound like work.

GOOD SAM

I was afraid this would come up. Don't you agree the financial rewards will be worth it?

LANDOWNER

Intellectually, yes. But emotionally, well, the deal I have now is so darn easy. They mail me a check, and I don't have to do or know anything. I'm so distant and unaccountable, it's like being a politician. But you have me rummaging around in a dusty old courthouse.

GOOD SAM

All right, that's a valid issue, so let's address it. How much time would you put into getting a lottery ticket that was guaranteed to win you $1 million?

LANDOWNER

A guaranteed $1 million lottery winner?

GOOD SAM

Yes. You'd do just about anything, wouldn't you?

LANDOWNER

Of course I would.

GOOD SAM

It would have your full attention? You'd be excited? You'd be very determined?

LANDOWNER

Yes, yes, yes. It would be one of the highlights of my life.

GOOD SAM

And you know that a winning $1 million lottery ticket pays $50,000 a year for 20 years, right?

LANDOWNER

Okay, I see what you're doing. My potential $48,000 a year from a billboard is almost as much. But it doesn't seem like the same thing. One's free, and the other isn't.

GOOD SAM

We're talking about a lot more than $48,000 a year.

LANDOWNER

How?

GOOD SAM

Annual rate increases. Not even counting production revenue, $48,000 increased by six percent for 20 years brings in over $1.8 million. Then it keeps paying, while lottery winnings end. And while not everyone will make that kind of money, the example is still legitimate. Now think for a moment. Is that better than the pizza money you're making from your current lease?

LANDOWNER

C'mon, don't make jokes.

GOOD SAM

Then let's get back to the original topic. You were whining.

LANDOWNER

I wasn't exactly whining.

GOOD SAM

Yes, you were. You said you have a great deal now because the billboard company mails you a check and you don't have to work for it, and then you said -

LANDOWNER

Okay, okay. I get your point.

GOOD SAM

Are you sure? Because I don't want to impose on you to get off your butt for nearly $2 million if you don't think it's worth it. Besides, I'm sure your current billboard company would be more than happy to keep that money if you're too lazy to go out and get it.

Chapter 14

LANDOWNER

Tell me more about the leases themselves.

GOOD SAM

We need to back up first. Something's bothering me, and I need to think it through.

LANDOWNER

What is it?

GOOD SAM

I owe you an apology.

LANDOWNER

For what?

GOOD SAM

A minute ago, you raised a good point. And I squashed you. The fact is, you were right, and I was wrong.

LANDOWNER

Why do you say that?

GOOD SAM

What I had initially envisioned was nothing less than a landowner uprising. I saw people reading this book, becoming informed, and taking action. But after hearing you, I'm not sure change is possible.

LANDOWNER

But there will be change. The amount of money involved is just too large. Give it another chance.

GOOD SAM

I don't think so. You were right when you said the landowners get free money for doing nothing. It would be a mistake to underestimate how powerful that is. Plus, my vision was flawed. Eight hundred thousand landowners are not going to wander the streets looking for each other like homeless, drooling zombies.

LANDOWNER

Maybe they will.

GOOD SAM

No they won't. Besides, the fact that many billboard landowners are businesses is both good and bad. It's good because it means many landowners are smart, successful individuals with corporate resources. It also means they'll be busy. Maybe too busy, even for the kind of money we're talking about.

LANDOWNER

But there are billions of dollars at stake!

GOOD SAM

I know. But that won't be enough. And even it it was, so what? The landowners don't know how to run billboard companies. It's harder than it looks. And even if they did, professionals could run them better.

LANDOWNER

I hadn't thought of that.

GOOD SAM

Besides, who among the landowners would be in charge? How would that be decided? How would they be paid? And how would the landowners know they weren't being taken advantage of by someone in their own group? So that's why I'm apologizing. My vision of a strong, smooth-running, multi-billion dollar industry magically emerging from 800,000 sleepy landowners is just plain silly.

LANDOWNER

Shoot. And we were so close. Isn't there a solution?

GOOD SAM

Maybe. That's what I've been mulling over. If the billboard industry is currently based upon the concept of free money for doing nothing, then someone else has to offer something better to the landowners. Something more powerful. Yet the Free Money simplicity of the old system will have to be maintained.

LANDOWNER

Is that possible?

GOOD SAM

I think so.

LANDOWNER

How?

GOOD SAM

The way I see it, the only concept that can overcome free money for doing nothing is MORE free money for doing nothing.

LANDOWNER

What do you mean?

GOOD SAM

I believe it's in the best interests of the landowners to have someone do everything for them. And I mean everything.

LANDOWNER

Can't the landowners do it all themselves?

GOOD SAM

They could try, but it would take far longer, and they'd be making things up as they went along. I think a particular danger is that some egocentric landowner who runs, say, an advertising agency or a commercial sign company, will step forward and claim that he or she is a billboard expert, and fully capable of being in charge.

LANDOWNER

Yeah, I could see that happening. Is that a bad idea?

GOOD SAM

It would be a disaster. And while the landowners could do everything, they would face a much higher degree of risk. But they don't have to. I have no doubt that a strong, experienced, well-financed management team could be assembled to do all the work for the landowners.

LANDOWNER

But they'd want to be paid for all that work.

GOOD SAM

Of course they would. And not just paid. They would expect to get rich. So would the initial investors. But I think it's the only way the landowners will get control of the outdoor advertising industry, should they choose to do so.

LANDOWNER

At the very least, it's the fastest way for change to occur.

GOOD SAM

You're right, and that's very significant. And as you pointed out, we're talking about billions of dollars here. Personally, I think the landowners are smart enough to give a percentage of that to the people who will do all the work.

LANDOWNER

Because the new system will give the landowners several times what they were getting before, yet they still won't have to do anything for it. It's more free money for doing nothing, just like you said.

GOOD SAM

Correct. And a professional management team will run the new company more profitably than the landowners could. I don't say that as a challenge, just as a fact, and it means the landowners will likely make more money with this option than if they tried to do it themselves anyway.

LANDOWNER

The option will pay for itself.

GOOD SAM

Of course it will. After all, someone will have to do the work. It sure isn't going to get done by itself. And don't forget that the landowners may be opposed every step of the way by gnarly old billboard companies who will be as tough to remove as tree roots.

LANDOWNER

How do you envision the new company and the landowners interacting?

GOOD SAM

I'd first make sure all the landowners read this book. That would be imperative, so everyone was on common ground. Then I'd have a meeting with representatives of both the landowners and the new company. I would make it clear that they're on the same side, and that their interests were aligned. Without that understanding, nothing else would make sense.

LANDOWNER

How would you explain it to everyone?

GOOD SAM

I'd turn to the new management team and say "Hey, don't be stupid. Don't disrespect the landowners. Don't try to hide secret clauses in fine print. Make sure the landowners are on the board of directors, and all finances are open for review. Work together, and everyone wins. If you put your interests ahead of the landowners, you'll fail. This is a great, great opportunity to create one of the world's best companies. Don't mess it up."

LANDOWNER

What would you say to the landowners?

GOOD SAM

I'd say "Hey, don't be stupid. The people in this new company are going to work hard to make you rich, and they're going to earn every dime. If you don't give them an environment where they can make serious money, they'll walk. If that happens, you'll have to replace them with incompetent goofballs who will run the new company into the ground. Then you'll have to replace those goofballs with new goofballs, and the downward spiral will have begun. So share some of the wealth, and you'll end up making a lot more money than if you hadn't."

LANDOWNER

That kind of direct talk may not make you very popular.

GOOD SAM

I totally disagree with that. Would you prefer the usual corporate blather, where lots of words are spoken but nothing gets said?

LANDOWNER

Well, no, but -

GOOD SAM

Hey, I have confidence in the intelligence of the landowners, and believe they would recognize truth and common sense when they heard it. It's that simple.

Chapter 15

LANDOWNER

How do the landowners start the process? And be specific.

GOOD SAM

At the absolute minimum, all the landowners should visit the Web site as soon as possible.

LANDOWNER

Because if enough landowners become informed quickly enough, it will freeze the industry and give the landowners time to organize.

GOOD SAM

Right. In fact, anyone who contacts the landowners, including the new prospective management teams, should begin by making sure all the landowners have visited the Web site and read this book.

LANDOWNER

Why?

GOOD SAM

For credibility. Otherwise, the prospective management teams, who have themselves read this book, would be accused of spooning out information to the landowners bit by bit, then asking the landowners to sign contracts. Once such duplicity was discovered, and I assure you it would be discovered, such people would be run out of town so fast their heads would spin.

LANDOWNER

I agree. And speaking as a landowner, I sure wouldn't give anyone a second chance. If someone is honest with me up front, I'll listen. But if someone tries to trick me and I find out about it, we're done forever. And I have a long memory.

GOOD SAM

I think your fellow landowners will feel the same way. That's why the only way for anyone to establish credibility and good will is to make sure all the landowners read this book. There's just no other way to do it without coming across as a common hustler trying to make a quick buck off someone else's work.

LANDOWNER

Okay, let's say that one way or another, all the landowners quickly read this book. Then what? How do you see things really getting started?

GOOD SAM

Here's what I would do. Let's say there's a market with, oh, 1000 landowners. I would contact all of them, but I'd find a dozen or so representative landowners to actually talk to. Call it an advisory board, consisting of 12 respected businesspeople who are all local billboard landowners.

LANDOWNER

Why just 12?

GOOD SAM

It doesn't have to be 12. It could be six, or ten. But it has to be a small group, or nothing will get done. Remember, there are probably going to be several competing management groups approaching the landowners. If all of them have to talk to all 1000 landowners, and each landowner has to have his or her attorney review the terms of each group, well, it turns into a big gooey mess.

LANDOWNER

There would be a lot of activity, but no progress.

GOOD SAM

All it would do is generate literally millions of dollars in attorney's fees. That's why I'd try to work with a respected, representative group of landowners who would carefully review the offer, while keeping the other landowners fully informed of the process. If the proposal was favorable, the group would endorse the plan. I would then hope that the other landowners would be smart enough to sign up.

LANDOWNER

Because if the 1000 landowners can't agree, they'll bicker like children and eventually break up into, say, ten competing billboard companies of 100 each. And a lot of the wonderful stuff we've been talking about would be gone.

GOOD SAM

True. Anyway, that's how I'd do it. Other people might have other ideas. Keep in mind, however, that some people in the old billboard industry might take steps to prevent all 1000 landowners from working together. If they can create distrust and uncertainty, it will be to their advantage.

LANDOWNER

That occurred to me, too. But even with advisory boards, how will the landowners evaluate the various offers? Without question, some of them will be from smooth-talking con men. And it wouldn't surprise me if some of the offers even came from shills controlled by the old billboard industry, with the goal of swaying us away from the ideas in this book. So even if we're smart businesspeople, and even if we have legal advice, who can we trust?

GOOD SAM

At some point, the deal has to ring true. It has to feel right. And that can only happen if both sides are fully informed. You'll even have the option of continuing to work with the same billboard company as before, only now as an organized group, and on much better terms.

LANDOWNER

The old billboard company? Forget it. Shifty once, shifty always, as my grandpop used to say.

GOOD SAM

Oh, I don't know. Don't they at least deserve a chance?

LANDOWNER

Not as far as I'm concerned. I may not be the smartest guy in the world, but I say that the old billboard companies have mistreated us for decades, and don't deserve a second chance under any circumstances. That's just my opinion, though.

GOOD SAM

Well, I suppose that question will have to be answered by each market's landowners.

Chapter 16

LANDOWNER

If you were part of a well-financed management team making a presentation to the landowners, how would you structure the deal?

GOOD SAM

Two steps. First, I would offer guaranteed payments to the landowners that equaled or exceeded their previous leases.

LANDOWNER

Guaranteed? No matter what?

GOOD SAM

Yes. That would eliminate risk for the landowners, and continue the flow of free money for doing nothing. Second, I would also offer shared revenue based upon certain levels. As the company made more money, the landowners would get more money, beyond their guaranteed lease payments. Naturally, all financials would be open to review.

LANDOWNER

What would you want in return?

GOOD SAM

The opportunity to earn money to compensate for the risk, the initial investment, and the ongoing work, and also equity to provide an incentive to grow the company's overall value. The key is that it would be a deal with aligned interests. That would either make sense to the landowners, or it wouldn't. If so, then great. Let's get started. If it didn't work out, hey, I'll bet you a doughnut the sun would still rise the next morning.

LANDOWNER

What would the ultimate goal be?

GOOD SAM

For who?

LANDOWNER

For everyone.

GOOD SAM

For a truly spectacular company, I think the ultimate goal would be a public stock offering, because it would create interesting merger opportunities.

LANDOWNER

Merger opportunities?

GOOD SAM

The billboard industry is currently undergoing rapid consolidation, and valuations are high because the sign companies are coveted by other communications groups who are suffering audience fragmentation in their own product lines. In a public company, the landowners would then make guaranteed money from their sites, plus have corporate equity and shareholder value potential.

LANDOWNER

That sounds ideal.

GOOD SAM

Perhaps more than you know, because I see billboards as only the first step of a very specific three-phase corporate development, with each succeeding phase larger than the prior one. Being a public company would make those steps easier.

LANDOWNER

Wait, wait, wait. Stop the presses. You're saying step one, the billboard phase, can be incredibly profitable, and worth a king's ransom. Yet step two would be larger than step one, and step three larger than step two? Is that what you meant to say?

GOOD SAM

Yes. And I'm not talking about just buying other media companies, although that might be part of it. What I have in mind is a bit more sophisticated. It would also be a tremendous amount of fun.

LANDOWNER

It sounds like you have the whole thing planned out.

GOOD SAM

I do. For each step, I see the corporate makeup, the offices, the personnel, the customers, the alliances, the work flow, the balance sheets, everything. It's as clear to me as a photograph.

LANDOWNER

Will you tell me right now?

GOOD SAM

Now isn't the time. But if the landowners succeed in phase one, perhaps someone will be interested. Eventually, it will be their decision to move forward or not.

LANDOWNER

That leads me to another question. Why didn't you do this on your own? You certainly sound like you know what you're talking about. Why didn't you write a business plan, go to venture capitalists, raise some money, and start a company that approached all the landowners in the way you describe?

GOOD SAM

Because it would have been impossible to keep secret, no matter how many non-disclosure papers were signed. So I came up with the idea of fully informing the landowners first, with the belief that as long as they were at the forefront, everything else would fall into place. Plus, I'm just a fictional character, which may have dissuaded some investors.

LANDOWNER

That's true. I forgot about that. But you know, there's a weakness to your plan.

GOOD SAM

What's that?

LANDOWNER

It's true that you've given all the landowners the opportunity to become informed, providing they put forth some tiny bit of effort to publicize things. But you've informed all the billboard companies, too. They'll surely read this book, and they'll know all our plans.

GOOD SAM

So what? I believe if the landowners organize and work together, the old billboard companies become pretty much irrelevant. It's sort of like a football game. Knowing an opponent's strategy and being able to stop it are two very different things.

Chapter 17

LANDOWNER

Since someone else will be doing all the work for the landowners, does that mean you and I don't have anything more to talk about?

GOOD SAM

Technically, you have to publicize this information first. Then someone else will do all the work. But you do have to take that important first step.

LANDOWNER

What about after that? Is there anything else I have to know?

GOOD SAM

Yes. The more the landowners know, the better their decisions will be. So let's just jump around on different subjects for awhile, and see where it leads us. Beyond that, the Web site will be essential, because there will be things we couldn't cover if we talked for a year.

LANDOWNER

Then tell me more about the leases themselves. Earlier, you said something about legally cancelling or not renewing the leases. Can it really be that easy?

GOOD SAM

Most people don't understand how fragile some billboard leases are. And while every billboard company is different, I heard of one company where over half the leases were for under one year, and over 95 percent were due to expire in less than four years.

LANDOWNER

Aren't all the leases on the same schedule?

GOOD SAM

No. They're staggered throughout the entire calender because they were signed one at a time over a period of years. However, many leases have cancellation clauses, which means a landowner can legally end the relationship with a simple letter of notification.

LANDOWNER

What percentage of leases have cancellation clauses?

GOOD SAM

I don't know.

LANDOWNER

What if my lease can't be cancelled, and it expires in, say, four years. Should I wait until then to join the other landowners?

GOOD SAM

No! Jeepers, I thought that was clear. You join the other landowners immediately, regardless of when your lease is due. Your clout only comes from a unified group.

LANDOWNER

Join immediately. Okay. But if I join the group, won't the billboard people just move my sign down the street? Then nothing changes for them, but I lose everything.

GOOD SAM

I'm glad you asked that, because threatening to move a billboard is an old tactic of the billboard industry. It's commonly used in negotiations to keep landowners obedient.

LANDOWNER

Is it a valid threat?

GOOD SAM

No. First, city zoning laws make it difficult, and often impossible, to erect new billboards in areas where billboards already exist. Second, if the billboard company could have built just down the road from you, it probably would have already done so. And third, the billboard company would have to move all the billboards, not just yours.

LANDOWNER

Because I'd be part of the united landowners group, and we would work together. I keep forgetting that.

GOOD SAM

Besides, the prospective new landowners would also have access to this book, which means moving billboards really isn't an option no matter how you look at it.

LANDOWNER

Then how might the billboard companies react once the landowners start to unite? After all, they're not going to quietly disappear, and we probably won't get away with writing memos that say "Thank you in advance for your cooperation."

GOOD SAM

Some of the mangier companies will bark predictable dogma with the hopes of hounding the landowners into poor decisions.

LANDOWNER

Those heels. They'll expect us to flee.

GOOD SAM

But the smart companies might quickly sell out to the landowners before they lose what little leverage they have.

LANDOWNER

What about the ones not smart enough to sell out to the landowners?

GOOD SAM

My guess is they will go on full alert the same week this book is published. Emergency meetings will be held as contracts are reviewed and risk is assessed. Then they'll put on the usual bluff and gruff.

LANDOWNER

Bluff and gruff? What's that?

GOOD SAM

Bluff, just like poker. They'll pretend they're not worried, and try to fool the landowners that the power hasn't really shifted. If that doesn't work, they'll switch to gruff, which means they'll try to intimidate anyone who stands up to them. But don't you fall for it. Bluff and gruff is nothing but a desperate ploy from a frightened bully.

LANDOWNER

Could it work?

GOOD SAM

No. It only works one on one. To a large, well-informed group, such false bravado is actually comical. However, some especially foolish billboard companies might try a two-front attack.

LANDOWNER

Like what?

GOOD SAM

First, they could try to sign landowners to new contracts before the landowners have a chance to read this book. Second, they could file some harassment lawsuits, just to jam things up.

LANDOWNER

New contracts, and lawsuits. Let's talk about each of those two subjects in more detail.

GOOD SAM

Okay, but let's talk about them in two separate chapters.

LANDOWNER

Why?

GOOD SAM

Studies have shown that modern readers have short attention spans, and breaking material into smaller segments enhances retention.

Chapter 18

LANDOWNER

Let's cover new contracts first. Would hurrying around and tricking landowners into new, unfair contracts be effective?

GOOD SAM

No. Billboard people can say anything they want. But it's by their actions that landowners will judge them. And because of that, any billboard company that rushes out to trick landowners into sneaky unfair contracts weeks or days or even hours before the landowners read this book will be obliterated. It's an incredibly dangerous and irreversible path of action.

LANDOWNER

Because honest billboard companies will have a chance to continue doing business with us. I guess we'll see, though, because some billboard companies will probably try to do exactly what we're describing.

GOOD SAM

But they'll get caught. Imagine a billboard manager who quickly goes to a landowner with a hasty new contract. Hiding his nervousness, he asks the landowner to sign. The landowner is quiet as a dark look comes over his face. Then he says "No, I don't think I will. And by the way, you insidious little creep, I read the book that you had hoped I hadn't read, and the author predicted you would try exactly what you're trying."

LANDOWNER

And after he threw the billboard guy out the door, the landowner would immediately start warning his fellow landowners about the evil billboard people and their nefarious schemes. Do you think some billboard companies will try anyway?

GOOD SAM

Probably. For some billboard people, the only reactions will be to mislead, bamboozle, and hoodwink.

LANDOWNER

All while being slicker than a greased pig's shadow, as my grandpop also used to say.

GOOD SAM

That's okay. Against organized landowners, such tactics are the exact opposite of what is required for the long-term health of the old billboard companies.

LANDOWNER

Long term health? Are you saying there's a way for the old billboard companies to survive everything we're talking about?

GOOD SAM

Not only survive, there is a way for them to grow into even stronger companies than they are now. But it doesn't involve flimflamming the landowners with unfair contracts.

LANDOWNER

Will you tell me what it does involve?

GOOD SAM

No.

LANDOWNER

Will the billboard companies think of it themselves?

GOOD SAM

No.

LANDOWNER

You're sure?

GOOD SAM

Yes.

LANDOWNER

Why?

GOOD SAM

They don't have the mindset for it. And even if I did tell them, it would be like explaining algebra to a group of parakeets. Their eyes would be open and their heads would nod, but nothing would sink in. They just wouldn't get it.

Chapter 19

LANDOWNER

Now let's talk about lawsuits. After all, this is America, where any vindictive old goober can hire a lawyer.

GOOD SAM

That's true. There was one owner who bragged that he had been in over 100 lawsuits, and that they had no impact on him at all.

LANDOWNER

Over 100 lawsuits? My gosh. Did he get mixed up in a lot of misunderstandings, or was he just some thug who hid behind legal henchmen?

GOOD SAM

I don't know. Nor can I predict what all billboard companies will do. But if they try to claim tortious interference it will backfire right in their faces.

LANDOWNER

What do turtles have to do with anything?

GOOD SAM

Not tortoise interference. Tortious.

LANDOWNER

Oh. Why will such an obviously baseless claim backfire, other than the fact that it's obviously baseless?

GOOD SAM

All I've said in this book is for landowners to explore their already existing options. They can either not renew their leases, or exercise existing cancellation clauses. Both those things happen all the time, all over the country. They are options the landowners have always had, but didn't fully understand.

LANDOWNER

Like Dorothy and her magic red slippers.

GOOD SAM

But a contract does not make it illegal for other people to approach one of the parties with an offer to be effective once the original contract is no longer valid. If such an action was contractual interference, billboard companies themselves would be guilty of it with every sales call they make.

LANDOWNER

Explain, please.

GOOD SAM

Billboard salespeople often try to convince potential advertising clients to stop using competitors such as radio, television, or newspaper. They even monitor those sources to create prospect lists. That means the very basis of billboard companies is to encourage the use of billboards over competing media in which the clients already, under contract, invest their money.

LANDOWNER

In other words, billboard companies themselves aggressively encourage potential clients to cancel or not renew contracts all the time. How interesting.

GOOD SAM

It is, isn't it? And if there was a trial, top economists would carry enough authority to more than nullify any puppets the billboard industry might pay to be so-called expert witnesses.

LANDOWNER

What do top economists say that might help us?

GOOD SAM

They use the phrase "creative destruction" to describe the strength and driving force of capitalism. It means a free market allows, and even requires, that superior technology and business models replace inferior technology and business models.

LANDOWNER

The way handheld calculators displaced slide rules. Or the way the telegraph eliminated the Pony Express.

GOOD SAM

Exactly. Creative destruction openly acknowledges that significant damage is inflicted upon the outdated institutions that can't, or won't, adapt. Real money is lost. Real companies go out of business. Entire industries fade away. Creative destruction may be harsh, but it's reality. It is also the bedrock of the United States economy. What it doesn't mean is that outside parties are liable when inferior industries struggle due to their own inherent weaknesses.

LANDOWNER

If your face is lopsided, don't blame the mirror.

GOOD SAM

Right again. If the old billboard companies experience problems, it's because of flaws in the business models which they created. In fact, I hereby challenge all billboard companies to give all their landowners full access to all financial information, and give their landowners the right to cancel leases at any time.

LANDOWNER

You know that won't happen.

GOOD SAM

I know nothing of the kind. There might be plenty of honest billboard companies that would welcome the opportunity to show integrity. All I'm doing is giving them a way to prove themselves. If they have nothing to hide, then they have nothing to fear. Why don't you think it will happen?

LANDOWNER

Because the current system is unfair.

GOOD SAM

That's your opinion. The billboard companies will say the current system is just dandy.

LANDOWNER

Okay. I see what you're doing. If the current system is fair, then the billboard companies have nothing to fear from accepting your challenge and proving you wrong. If they don't accept your challenge, they're admitting the system is unfair, and that they have something to hide. That's a trap they can't get out of.

GOOD SAM

It's not a trap. It's a challenge. Whether any billboard companies accept it is up to them.

Chapter 20

LANDOWNER

Will the billboard companies try to sway public opinion in order to generate sympathy or support?

GOOD SAM

Maybe. If they do, they might try to quote some possibly bogus figures about how much public service billboard space they've donated over the years.

LANDOWNER

Public service?

GOOD SAM

Billboards that were supposedly donated to nonprofit organizations.

LANDOWNER

Is a lot of money involved?

GOOD SAM

For some markets, the figure might be in the millions of dollars if several years or more are counted.

LANDOWNER

How might billboard companies try to use this to their advantage?

GOOD SAM

By trying to garner public sympathy and claiming to be good corporate citizens. And please note that I'm not in any way saying billboard companies don't ever perform legitimate public service. But sometimes what they claim isn't always what it seems.

LANDOWNER

How so?

GOOD SAM

Donated billboard space is often a great benefit to the billboard company. First, the billboard company may secretly make plenty of money on production. Second, especially in the case of posters, billboard companies often use the nonprofit designs on a space available basis.

LANDOWNER

Space available. What does that mean?

CHARITY BILLBOARDS

GOOD SAM

Space available posters mean the billboard company uses them, if at all, whenever and wherever they want to use them. For example, a nonprofit group buys 50 posters at a greatly inflated price. Then the billboard company has total control as to where and when those posters go up, and for how long. No guarantees.

LANDOWNER

That doesn't sound like such a good deal for the charity.

GOOD SAM

Often it isn't, because some billboard companies just use the posters to cover up their own paying clients that have to be covered anyway. Say there's a paid billboard that promoted a July sale. Well, that looks pretty goofy in August. So it has to be covered. The same goes for weather-damaged posters. Those too have to be covered right away, until a paying client can go up.

LANDOWNER

So the public service billboards are actually to the advantage of the billboard companies.

GOOD SAM

Sometimes. But whenever some billboard companies need instant public relations regarding community involvement, they add up the supposed value of all those public service billboards based on the open rate card. And bingo! They look like angels.

LANDOWNER

And if anyone opposes billboards, the billboard people just show a picture of, say, an anti-cancer sign, implying that anyone who is against billboards is pro-cancer.

GOOD SAM

That's exactly what happens. And it's very effective. It's shut down many anti-billboard discussions over the years, because no politician wants to be perceived as being against any of the legitimate nonprofit organizations the billboard companies hide behind. It's a truly brilliant strategy.

LANDOWNER

Scummy, but brilliant.

Chapter 21

LANDOWNER

Could a billboard company start over by buying land for future billboards? That way, they would eliminate their leasing problems forever.

GOOD SAM

No, because the price of properly zoned land would increase once billboard companies started to buy it. Real estate agents all over the country would study plat books and zoning laws to know if a spot could have billboards.

LANDOWNER

Then the owner could either put up his own sign, or dramatically increase the price of the land and make it available to the highest bidder.

[Handwritten margin note: BUYING LAND / BILLBOARDS = TAXES]

GOOD SAM

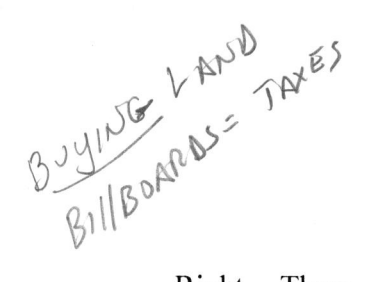

Right. There would be free-market competition which automatically adjusted to whatever the billboard industry did. The more determined the billboard companies became to buy land, the higher the prices would go. There would be annual property taxes, too.

LANDOWNER

It would be a staggering amount of money.

GOOD SAM

But even if they could spend that kind of money, there just isn't enough properly zoned land available. So no matter how you approach the problem, billboard companies cannot go out and buy land for their signs.

LANDOWNER

Gee, I really don't see any good options for the old billboard companies. If this were a game of poker, it sounds like the landowners have all the aces.

GOOD SAM

If they make smart decisions, the landowners have the whole deck.

Chapter 22

LANDOWNER

It sounds like the landowners have nothing to worry about.

GOOD SAM

Not quite. We haven't talked about the most serious threat that could stop everything.

LANDOWNER

You mean there's still a way the old billboard companies could win and the landowners could lose?

GOOD SAM

Sort of. Long term, the only way the landowners can lose is through indifference, or if they live down to their reputations of being stupid and lazy.

LANDOWNER

What about the short term?

GOOD SAM

Billboard companies could give millions of dollars to politicians to strip the landowners of their rights.

LANDOWNER

Whoa. Can they do that?

GOOD SAM

They can try.

LANDOWNER

That sounds illegal.

GOOD SAM

It won't be, and there are people in the billboard industry who have experience in influencing government regulations. I heard the billboard industry is behind only defense contractors and the tobacco industry in certain types of political contributions.

LANDOWNER

They bribe lawmakers.

GOOD SAM

I didn't say that.

LANDOWNER

Then maybe I'm missing something. The billboard people give money to lawmakers. And the billboard people get favors in return. How is that different from a bribe?

GOOD SAM

I don't know. But it's how America works.

LANDOWNER

What should we do about it?

GOOD SAM

Take advantage of your own overwhelming numbers, and keep special watch on lawmakers involved with billboard legislation. While you're at it, you should certainly hire your own lobbyists. Locally, get to know your city council members. At the state level, know your senators and representatives. Meet with them. Make your numbers felt. Nationally, you'll need some well-connected people in Washington DC.

LANDOWNER

How much will all that cost?

GOOD SAM

I don't know, but if 800,000 landowners each chip in three dollars a month, you'll have nearly $29 million a year to lobby with. That will quickly turn the landowners into one of the most powerful political groups in the country.

LANDOWNER

Do you really think so?

GOOD SAM

Absolutely. You'll have money, motivation, existing rights, and huge numbers of people. Any politician that fights you will be seen as being against farmers, minorities, small businesses, retirees, strong local tax bases, personal property rights, and maybe against the spirit of America itself.

LANDOWNER

Why do you mention those types of people?

GOOD SAM

Because they're all in the mix of the 800,000 landowners. Take farmers for example. For many of them, control of their own billboard might mean the difference between financial success or ruin.

LANDOWNER

What about small businesses?

GOOD SAM

Many, maybe even most, billboards are on land owned by small businesses. If you drive through any city and look at where the billboards are placed, you'll see what I mean. And by the way, when I use the figure of 800,000 landowners, I'm not even allowing for spouses, or business co-owners. Calculate it that way, and the number of legitimate billboard landowners is well into the millions.

LANDOWNER

Since it's accurate, why not use the higher number all the time? It sounds so impressive.

GOOD SAM

It does, but it might confuse people into thinking there are millions of billboards, which there aren't. Instead, I used the more conservative 800,000 figure to denote primary decision makers. But there's no doubt the real number of true landowners is several times that figure, because of joint ownership.

LANDOWNER

Millions of landowners. Wow. And they come from all walks of life. That diversity gives the landowners a lot of power, doesn't it?

GOOD SAM

Yes, and they'll keep that power unless it's taken away from them in secret lawmaking sessions where protectionist legislation is hidden in small print and slipped into bills before anyone knows about it.

LANDOWNER

Boy, I hate secret protectionist legislation. It's like a silent you-know-what in a movie theater. Everyone eventually smells what happened, and no one is pleased about it. What if there is such legislation? What should we do?

GOOD SAM

Find a way around it until you can vote the dishonest politicians out of office and replace them with ethical people who will rescind the unfair laws.

LANDOWNER

How could we get around it?

GOOD SAM

Just be smart. Let's say a law was passed that said the landowners -

LANDOWNER

The millions of landowners.

GOOD SAM

- right, the millions of landowners, could not have billboards on their own property, and that the signs had to be owned by some other billboard company.

LANDOWNER

That law wouldn't make any sense.

GOOD SAM

No, it wouldn't. Unless you're one of the old billboard companies. But all you'd have to do is get a bunch of landowners together. Half would be from one side of town, and half from the other side. Then you would form two separate companies and lease billboards on each other's land. You'd then agree to a formula that recognized different rates, and everyone wins.

LANDOWNER

And we'd still be obeying the law.

GOOD SAM

Yes. But if you do run into protectionist legislation, here are two things that might help you. First, many billboard companies have a few billboards on their own land, usually at their main offices.

LANDOWNER

Wait a second. Stop right there. If the billboard companies have billboards on their own land, why can't the landowners?

GOOD SAM

That's a good question.

LANDOWNER

Is it just a matter of incorporating as a billboard company? Because if it is, I can get that done in less than an hour.

GOOD SAM

Maybe it is that easy. I don't know. But the second thing you should know is that many landowners currently receive free billboard usage instead of lease money.

LANDOWNER

They get their payment in trade? Why?

GOOD SAM

Many of the landowners want to advertise on billboards. But they weren't allowed to put up their own billboards because that would have been on-premise signage, which is often not allowed by legislation that was influenced by billboard companies.

LANDOWNER

Wait a second. A landowner can't own his own billboard to advertise his own business, but a billboard company can own a billboard in the same spot to advertise someone else's business?

GOOD SAM

Kinda goofy, isn't it?

LANDOWNER

Why should the government legislate advertising content in a fashion that is exclusively biased against landowners?

GOOD SAM

Again, I don't know. Perhaps such protectionist legislation is even unconstitutional on the grounds of free speech. But I don't know if anyone has ever challenged it from that perspective.

LANDOWNER

Boy, I hope the politicians originally involved in that legislation enjoyed their money.

GOOD SAM

I couldn't say. Now there will be other things that come along. Some will be big, some will be small. But there will always be solutions. Always. And whether their total size is 800,000 or eight million, that's something the voting landowners, and their friends, and their families, and their business associates, should remember.

Chapter 23

GOOD SAM

I'd like to add a brief footnote to our last chapter.

LANDOWNER

What about?

GOOD SAM

One time I read an article about billboards, and the writer talked to a spokesperson for the outdoor advertising industry. The writer asked how many billboards exist in the country. The spokesperson replied that there are around 400,000 billboards on federal highways in the United States. For the rest of their conversation, the writer then talked as if there were 400,000 billboards total. The spokesperson never corrected the error.

LANDOWNER

What error? Didn't the spokesperson say there were 400,000 billboards total?

GOOD SAM

No. As alert readers have already noticed, he said there were 400,000 billboards on federal highways.

LANDOWNER

Oh, I see. There are plenty of billboards that aren't on federal highways. Why was the spokesperson so misleading?

GOOD SAM

I don't know. It was especially odd because it was such an insignificant question.

LANDOWNER

Are the billboard people ashamed of their business? Are they afraid of what will happen if the public knew there were a million billboards in the country? Or are some billboard people naturally deceptive because it's how they conduct themselves all the time?

GOOD SAM

I don't know. But it's something you should keep in mind whenever you deal with someone in the billboard industry.

Chapter 24

LANDOWNER

If it's okay with you, I'd like to change directions now. What I want to discuss is sort of gossipy, but I think it's important.

GOOD SAM

I'm not sure what you mean.

LANDOWNER

One time I, a fictional character, was at a bar. I overheard several billboard managers talking about their business, and there were a lot of odd snippets that I didn't understand. In no particular order, could you explain some of them to me, with the understanding that they don't necessarily represent all billboard people or billboard companies?

GOOD SAM

Bar talk? Are you sure you want to do this?

LANDOWNER

Like I said, I think it's important.

GOOD SAM

Well, okay. I'll try.

LANDOWNER

Thanks. First, what's a mink farm?

GOOD SAM

One national billboard company had a CEO and a CFO, both males, who openly referred to a particular branch with predominately female employees as a mink farm. They thought they were being clever in a good old boy sort of way. Pretty soon, it spread throughout the company. Encouraged by this corporate attitude, a general manager hit on a young sales rep, then fired her when she refused to go for an afternoon romp in his downtown condo.

LANDOWNER

I bet there are some sexual harassment lawyers who would fail to see the humor in that.

GOOD SAM

I couldn't say. But it does show that such things start at the top work their way down. What else did you hear?

LANDOWNER

Bird nests?

GOOD SAM

At least one manager gave standing instructions to his on-site workers to always tear down bird nests from billboards, regardless if there were eggs or even baby birds in the nests. So the workers did just that, and the baby birds were left to die in the hot sun as the parent birds watched. Sometimes the workers showed their remorse by stomping the birds to death with their work boots. So the birds wouldn't suffer.

LANDOWNER

That's sick. What about blackboards? They used that term like it was some sort of product.

GOOD SAM

Sometimes tobacco and alcohol companies liked to advertise on billboards in poor neighborhoods for the purpose of pushing cigarettes and spiked booze to economically lower-class minorities. Some people in the billboard industry openly called such signs blackboards.

LANDOWNER

They were racists.

GOOD SAM

To be fair, no, I don't think they were. The general attitude was that as long as the targeted people were poor and uneducated, it didn't matter what color their skin was.

LANDOWNER

They also talked about a widow, and laughed a lot. What does a widow have to do with billboards?

GOOD SAM

One story was about a billboard general manager who was in a protracted rate negotiation with a landowner.

LANDOWNER

Did the landowner want more money?

GOOD SAM

Yes, and talks had gone on for weeks. Then the landowner suddenly died one night, and two weeks later the billboard manager had the widow sign a lease that was for less than what the old rate had been.

LANDOWNER

Less? Why did she do that?

GOOD SAM

The billboard manager told the widow her dead husband had agreed to the reduction before he died, and pressured her to keep her husband's word on the deal. He even threatened to sue and tie up the estate if necessary.

LANDOWNER

He couldn't have tied up the estate. No way.

GOOD SAM

The widow didn't know that.

LANDOWNER

That's disgusting. What about collusion? The billboard guys whispered about that for a long time.

GOOD SAM

If a landowner tried to start a bidding war between or among competing billboard companies, sometimes the billboard managers would secretly compare bids to keep the lease amount low. The usual agreement was that no billboard company would interfere with another company's lease.

LANDOWNER

That's illegal, isn't it?

GOOD SAM

Beats me. You'll have to ask someone else that question. Did you hear anything else from the billboard guys at the bar?

LANDOWNER

Yeah, I did. There were a lot of personal stories. A lot of them. They even talked about one skirtchasing owner who -

GOOD SAM

Be careful.

LANDOWNER

Uh, now that I think about it, maybe it's not appropriate that we discuss that here.

GOOD SAM

Good choice.

LANDOWNER

But when the waitress brought the guys their bill, one of them looked her over and said "Honey, we're in the billboard business, and our erections are guaranteed to last 30 days, even in bad weather. What do you think of that?"

Chapter 25

LANDOWNER

I want to know more.

GOOD SAM

What did you have in mind?

LANDOWNER

Any negative stories that would show what kind of people we might, but not necessarily would, be dealing with. Sort of like the guys in the bar we talked about a minute ago.

GOOD SAM

That's an odd request. Why negative stories?

LANDOWNER

Because all the good and honest billboard people don't pose a threat to the landowners. At the very least, we'll be able to deal with them in a professional, ethical manner. There are such people in the industry, aren't there?

GOOD SAM

Of course there are. I heard of one aging owner who tried to sell his family-built billboard company to his employees for less than market value. The employees weren't able to raise the millions of dollars required, so he sold to a big national company instead. But his heart was in the right place, and he really did try.

LANDOWNER

See, that's a nice story. And there are probably more just like it. But if, on the other hand, there are sneaky billboard people out there, even if they're just the tiniest sliver of the total, I want to know about some of the things they've allegedly done so I might better recognize them if and when the time comes.

GOOD SAM

I see what you mean. But we have to get something clear first. I can't give you a percentage of how many billboard people are honest and dishonest. No one can. I can't even define those terms to everyone's agreement. All I can do is tell you stories, with the understanding that, like this entire book, the stories do not necessarily relate to all billboard people or billboard companies. Agreed?

LANDOWNER

Of course. It's like, oh, watching the television news. Just because there are stories about car wrecks doesn't mean everyone had a car wreck that day. No reasonable person would think that.

GOOD SAM

Okay. Then let's start with trees. As you can guess, some people in the billboard industry don't like certain trees, because they block their billboards. That conflict has led to some interesting events.

LANDOWNER

I bet.

GOOD SAM

The first story is about a market that was so widespread it took a couple of hours to drive from one side to the other. One day, the general manager sent an employee to cut down a tree that was blocking a billboard. But when the guy finally arrived at the site, he saw lots of trees and didn't know which one to cut.

LANDOWNER

What did he do?

GOOD SAM

He cut down a dozen trees, including mature oaks and pines.

LANDOWNER

Did the billboard company own the land?

GOOD SAM

No. The trees were on government land.

LANDOWNER

Did he get in trouble for it?

GOOD SAM

No. The cutter was praised by the manager for his quick thinking. By cutting down all the trees, he saved the company gas money. The billboard company also left the trees where they fell, knowing that tax dollars would pay for highway crews to clean up the mess. Then they raised the advertising rate on the billboard because it wasn't obstructed any more.

LANDOWNER

Amazing. What's the next tree story?

GOOD SAM

A billboard guy had just cut down a magnificent blue spruce when an elderly couple rushed from their nearby home. They were horrified at what had just been done.

LANDOWNER

Why?

GOOD SAM

Because the tree was on their land. As the woman cried, the husband shouted that they had planted the tree on their wedding day over sixty years earlier.

LANDOWNER

How did the billboard guy react?

GOOD SAM

He just explained that their dumb old tree blocked his company's nice new billboard. He didn't understand what all the fuss was about. Meanwhile, sap dripped out of the tree like blood, and the poor woman cried with gasping sobs.

LANDOWNER

Wasn't there anything the elderly couple could do about it? Couldn't they have sued or something?

GOOD SAM

If you were that age, would you want to get mired in a lawsuit against a rich corporation? Is that how you'd want to spend your time and energy?

LANDOWNER

I guess not.

GOOD SAM

The last tree story is about an irate landowner who called a general manager to complain that a billboard crew had almost cut down a tree on his property. The only reason the tree hadn't been cut was because the landowner caught the cutters as they were setting up their equipment. The landowner's call made the general manager angry.

LANDOWNER

Because his crew almost made a big mistake?

GOOD SAM

It was no mistake. The manager had instructed the crew to cut down the tree.

LANDOWNER

Then what was he mad about?

GOOD SAM

Three things. First, the crew had been told to go after dark. Second, the crew had been caught before they cut the tree instead of after. And third, the manager was livid that the landowner was so selfish. "I'm trying to run a business here," the billboard manager said. "I just don't understand people who only see things from their point of view."

LANDOWNER

He didn't see the irony of that statement?

GOOD SAM

No. He was dead-on serious.

LANDOWNER

Do you think the billboard managers in these three stories eventually regretted some of their actions?

GOOD SAM

No. They and their cronies joked about these stories. They thought it was especially funny when one manager stooped over and made his hands tremble when he imitated how the elderly woman had cried. "Boo-hoo-hoo, you killed our tree," he said. "Boo-hoo-hoo."

Chapter 26

LANDOWNER

Are there any stories about how some billboard companies may have treated some of their advertising clients?

GOOD SAM

Oh, sure. Perhaps a client would pay for 30 billboards, but only 15 would go up. Or a client would buy a 90-day campaign, but it would only run for 60 days. Or a manager would sell tree-blocked locations to out-of-town clients, and laugh because the worthless billboards "looked good on a map." But one of my favorites is the time an out-of-town client called a general manager and told him he was arriving the next day to ride the market.

LANDOWNER

Ride the market. What does that mean?

GOOD SAM

Riding the market is when the client drives around the city and looks at each individual billboard. It's usually done for large, multi-location campaigns.

LANDOWNER

Why would a client do that?

GOOD SAM

To make sure he wasn't cheated.

LANDOWNER

Oh, okay. What happened in this case?

GOOD SAM

Well, the display period for his billboards was almost over, but the client wanted to check their condition and take some pictures. Unfortunately, the billboards had never been posted.

LANDOWNER

Oops!

GOOD SAM

So the general manager had his entire crew drop everything else and post the locations that afternoon and early evening. During the next day's ride, the client was told the locations had been up the whole time. The general manager even accepted the client's praise.

LANDOWNER

Praise? What for?

GOOD SAM

Because the posters looked so fresh and new.

LANDOWNER

But they were fresh and new!

GOOD SAM

The client didn't know that, and he told the general manager how nice everything looked and how pleased he was.

LANDOWNER

Did the billboard manager keep a straight face?

GOOD SAM

Without blinking an eye, he said "Well, that's how we run things around here." After the happy client left, however, the billboard manager was upset.

LANDOWNER

Why?

GOOD SAM

Because the market ride made him miss his tee time, and the posting labor cut into that month's profit.

Chapter 27

LANDOWNER

Are there any more client stories?

GOOD SAM

I'll give you two more. The first involves a national rep firm.

LANDOWNER

What's a rep firm?

GOOD SAM

It's a company that represents national advertising clients for what are usually multi-market billboard campaigns. Rep firms bridge the gap between large national clients and local billboard companies. It's a very valuable service, and quite legitimate.

LANDOWNER

They work for the clients, not the billboard companies?

GOOD SAM

Right.

LANDOWNER

How do the relationships work?

GOOD SAM

A rep firm gets an agreement with an advertising client. A budget is committed. Then the rep firm contacts the various billboard companies in different markets and places the orders. That includes agreeing to locations, handling designs, ordering paper, and doing the billing.

LANDOWNER

What do the rep firms charge their clients for all that work?

GOOD SAM

Sometimes nothing.

LANDOWNER

Then how do they make money?

GOOD SAM

What's sometimes supposed to happen is that a rep firm takes a commission, say ten percent, of the space costs. That commission is deducted from what is paid to the billboard companies.

LANDOWNER

That sounds like a good deal for everyone. The clients get good service, the billboard companies get easy business, and the rep firms earn ten percent. And the client doesn't pay anything extra. Everybody wins.

GOOD SAM

Sometimes.

LANDOWNER

Is there a problem with that system?

GOOD SAM

I've heard of inflated rate cards just for the rep firms. Those rate cards are at least ten percent higher than the local rates.

LANDOWNER

Gee, that sounds deceitful. Do the clients know about this?

GOOD SAM

I believe most national clients think the rep firm is being paid out of the billboard company's share, not through secret inflated rates.

LANDOWNER

What do you think such billboard people would do if their actions were discovered? Would they apologize and return the ill-gotten money, with interest? Or would they scurry and hide like cockroaches when a light was turned on?

GOOD SAM

That's not for me to say. Perhaps some clients should review their records, however, and start asking their own questions.

Chapter 28

LANDOWNER

You said you had two more client stories. What's the second one?

GOOD SAM

I'll have to use some industry language with this one. The story is about a billboard company that allegedly overcharged poster clients by inflating the number of billboards required in a showing. You may not find this particularly riveting, but there are lots of advertising clients who will.

LANDOWNER

What's a showing?

GOOD SAM

A showing is a group of 12 x 24 foot poster billboards that run all at the same time.

LANDOWNER

A saturation campaign.

GOOD SAM

Yes. Showings come in four standard sizes called a 25 showing, a 50 showing, a 75 showing, and a 100 showing.

LANDOWNER

Does that mean there are 50 billboards in a 50 showing?

GOOD SAM

That sounds logical, but no, that's not what it means. The four numbers represent percentages of a city's population that can be reached on a daily basis with the group of billboards.

LANDOWNER

Huh?

GOOD SAM

A 50 showing generates a 50 percent daily reach of a city's population. A 75 showing generates a 75 percent daily reach. It's how the client determines the desired level of saturation.

TRAFFIC COUNTS

LANDOWNER

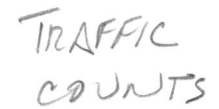

Okay. So how many billboards are in, say, a 50 showing?

GOOD SAM

That depends on the city. In a small town, a 50 showing might only require one or two billboards. In a large city, it might require several dozen.

LANDOWNER

What's the average?

GOOD SAM

There's no such thing. A showing's quantity is unique to every city.

LANDOWNER

But who decides how big a showing is, and how do they come up with the numbers?

GOOD SAM

Showing sizes are dictated by audited traffic counts.

LANDOWNER

You mean like those black cables that sometimes lay across roads and click when cars drive over them?

GOOD SAM

Yes. Those are traffic counters. Once those numbers are compiled, it's easy to relate them to a city's population and create accurate showing sizes.

LANDOWNER

But why have showings at all?

GOOD SAM

Without some sort of standardization, buying billboards in multiple cities would be almost impossible.

LANDOWNER

Do the rep firms use them?

GOOD SAM

Everyone uses them. Local clients, direct national clients, rep firms, and advertising agencies.

LANDOWNER

Oh, I get it. That means a media buyer can call 20 different billboard companies and get the rates for a standard 50 showing in 20 different cities.

GOOD SAM

Right. That buyer would still get 20 different-sized 50 showings, but at least there would be a basis for comparison, because each showing would generate 50 rating points a day.

LANDOWNER

Rating points?

GOOD SAM

Gross rating points, or GRPs. Fifty points means 50 percent of the population. It's easy.

LANDOWNER

Got it. And let me guess this story. A billboard company lied about the showing sizes, and didn't deliver on what was promised. Right?

GOOD SAM

Wrong. Instead, they lied about the number of billboards required for each showing. For example, when a client bought a 25 showing with the expectation of 25 points a day, what they actually got was a showing that generated 100 points a day. Sometimes even 200 points. The numbers the client expected and what they got weren't even close.

LANDOWNER

You've lost me. Why should a client be upset at getting more than what was expected?

GOOD SAM

This is very subtle, so I'll try to make it clear. If all the clients got showings that were several hundred percent larger than what they asked for, it means they could have bought far fewer billboards to meet their marketing needs.

LANDOWNER

Let's use an example. A buyer wanted a 50 showing in some city, and it took, say, 30 billboards to achieve that coverage.

GOOD SAM

Okay.

LANDOWNER

You're saying that the client might have been able to buy just five billboards to achieve a 50 showing, instead of 30 billboards.

GOOD SAM

Exactly.

LANDOWNER

So the client overpaid because he bought 25 more billboards than he needed.

GOOD SAM

Right. And that money could have either been saved by the client, placed in other markets, or put into other media for a more well-rounded campaign. But the client didn't know those options existed.

LANDOWNER

But didn't the billboard company's rate card list the average traffic counts next to each showing?

GOOD SAM

Yes. But the numbers on the rate card didn't match the actual numbers generated by the real showings.

LANDOWNER

Where did the rate card numbers come from?

GOOD SAM

The billboard company made them up.

LANDOWNER

Why?

GOOD SAM

Because it's a lot easier to sell five different clients 30 billboards each than it is to sell 30 clients five billboards each.

LANDOWNER

It's also sounds dishonest. You'd think the clients would have been smart enough to get the traffic counts in writing.

GOOD SAM

They did.

LANDOWNER

They knew they were getting all that wasted coverage?

GOOD SAM

It wasn't called wasted coverage. It was called bonus circulation.

LANDOWNER

Bonuses of several hundred percent? To everyone? C'mon, who's kidding who?

GOOD SAM

The billboard people would tell the client "Hey, we're giving all the other clients normal showings based on our rate card, but we're giving you this special big one because we like you so much."

LANDOWNER

They were giving them the big one all right.

GOOD SAM

Now, let's be nice.

LANDOWNER

Nice? The billboard company claimed the rate card was accurate when in fact everyone got showings that were several times larger than they needed to be. That means the rate card was a lie, printed with the corporate logo on it. That's fraud, isn't it?

GOOD SAM

I don't know the legal definition of fraud.

LANDOWNER

Then let me give it a try. The rate card was a lie, right?

GOOD SAM

It was inaccurate.

LANDOWNER

And the billboard people knew it was a lie?

GOOD SAM

They were aware of the inaccuracies. In fact, they created the inaccuracies, then used them as selling tools to close deals.

LANDOWNER

Which in turn resulted in great financial windfalls for the billboard company. If that's not fraud, I don't know what is. But why didn't the clients just buy the billboards they needed and let the billboard company keep the rest?

GOOD SAM

Because the buyers trusted the billboard company. More importantly, the billboard company required minimum buys, and wouldn't let clients pick and choose locations they needed.

LANDOWNER

Do you think clients would be upset if they ever found about about this? And do you think faked rate cards would be grounds for class action lawsuits? And would those lawsuits involve tens of millions of dollars in overcharges?

GOOD SAM

I don't know. Maybe we'll find out someday.

Chapter 29

LANDOWNER

How do billboard companies treat their own employees?

GOOD SAM

I couldn't say how all billboard companies treat all their employees. My guess is some companies treat their employees well, and others not so well. I could tell you a few stories about how some employees were treated, as long as you understand that such stories are not necessarily representative of the whole industry.

LANDOWNER

Consider it understood.

GOOD SAM

Are you sure? If I told you that one company president said the only reason he didn't replace his workers with trained monkeys was because the monkeys would want more money, would you understand it didn't necessarily represent all billboard company presidents?

LANDOWNER

Yes. If you were to say that.

GOOD SAM

Okay. Well, one company had a little trick whereby managers would set sales quotas so high that the total of all the salespeople's personal budgets added up to more than the company's billboard capacity. That meant it was impossible for all the salespeople to meet their goals, and guaranteed failure for a certain percentage of them. And failure resulted in termination.

LANDOWNER

Why would a manager do that?

GOOD SAM

One quote was "If you want to keep ten dogs mean, only give them enough food for eight. Nature will take care of the rest."

LANDOWNER

So some of them were set up to fail from the day they were hired, which would have impacted their families, their careers, everything. What a vicious thing to do.

GOOD SAM

But even managers had their troubles. One general manager left a billboard company and had to threaten to sue in order to get his $300,000 bonus.

LANDOWNER

Was there a dispute over the money?

GOOD SAM

No. Everything was in writing, and there was no disagreement. His former company just didn't feel like paying it, and wanted to see if the guy had the guts to fight them for it.

LANDOWNER

They just didn't feel like paying it. Darn it, that's not right. What's the difference between not paying that man his $300,000 and going to a bank and stealing $300,000?

GOOD SAM

I don't know. But trying to cheat people who have been loyal to you is certainly an odd way to run a company.

LANDOWNER

What about the other workers in a billboard company, like painters and bill posters and crane operators? Are there any stories about them?

GOOD SAM

Because of new technology, there are now far fewer painters in the industry than there were several years ago. But once, there was a group of billboard painters who didn't get overtime pay, even though they often worked 60 or 70 or even 80-hour weeks. It was a shame, because they were incredibly talented artists, and deserved better.

LANDOWNER

Why didn't they get overtime pay?

GOOD SAM

Because their company made them falsify their time cards to always say 40 hours per week. Then the painters were paid on a square-foot basis instead of hourly. That allowed the company to hire fewer painters, because the painters they did have had to work double shifts to meet their quotas.

LANDOWNER

So if a painter only worked 40-hour weeks, he or she wouldn't get enough work done to stay employed. Did the billboard company get away with that?

GOOD SAM

So far. But if anyone ever chose to investigate, they'd find that the time cards don't match up with the weekly payroll records.

LANDOWNER

Oh, I get it. If someone was paid on an hourly basis for consistent 40-hour weeks, the weekly pay should remain steady.

But the paychecks fluctuated greatly from week to week. If someone found the paper trail, there would be no excuse for that fluctuation, and the pernicious perpetrators would look like a bunch of clodpoll noddies. At least, that's what my -

GOOD SAM

- grandpop used to say. Right. Anyway, another time a billposter shattered his leg when he fell from a billboard due to improper training and faulty equipment. While he was in the hospital, the company president discussed firing him and replacing him with someone new who would cost less money.

LANDOWNER

Did that happen?

GOOD SAM

No. Instead, the president said he hoped the man's injuries were severe enough so he couldn't return to work. That way, the man could be replaced without fear of a lawsuit.

LANDOWNER

He hoped the man was injured seriously? The company president said that?

GOOD SAM

Hey, private jets are expensive, and every dollar counts.

LANDOWNER

What a creep.

GOOD SAM

Then there's the story about the nice manager who was concerned about long-term toxic effects on the painters. He requested professional breathing masks and improved room ventilation as protection from, among other things, both the lead-based paint fumes themselves, and also the lead dust that was created when the boards were scraped and sanded for re-use.

LANDOWNER

To whom was this request made?

GOOD SAM

The company president.

LANDOWNER

What was the answer?

GOOD SAM

He refused. "By definition," he said, "long-term effects don't show up for a long time. If those people are sick 20 years from now, it's not going to be my problem."

LANDOWNER

Not his problem.

GOOD SAM

Then, that same day, the president held a staff meeting and praised the workers for being valued members of the billboard company's "family."

Chapter 30

GOOD SAM

I want to switch gears now to talk about advertising clients for a moment. If you'll give me a little latitude, I'll get to my main point after I tell you two short stories.

LANDOWNER

Hey, I like your stories. Fire away.

GOOD SAM

The first story is about an advertising agency that lost at least $60 million in billings because of a goofed-up $10 project. Well, not just because of a $10 project. But that was the pebble that started the avalanche.

LANDOWNER

What happened?

GOOD SAM

One of the agency's clients wanted a copy made of a photographic slide.

LANDOWNER

That sounds easy enough.

GOOD SAM

It is easy. But when the agency's creative director made a copy, the client rejected it because the colors didn't match. So he tried again, and the client rejected it again. Frustrated at his inability to properly do the work, and openly cursing the client for being so persnickety, the art guy then had two copies made, and presented them to the client as the original and a copy.

LANDOWNER

He lied to the client.

GOOD SAM

And billed the client for work that wasn't approved. But his biggest mistake was that he thought his little trick was quite humorous, and he told the story to a lot of people, including another of the agency's clients.

LANDOWNER

He bragged to a client about what he had done? Did this art guy have "I'm an idiot!" tattooed to his forehead, or did he assume people would figure that out once they got to know him?

GOOD SAM

I can't say. But the story spread, and other clients didn't think it was so funny. They decided if the art guy was untruthful about something as small as a slide, he would be even worse about larger and more expensive things.

LANDOWNER

Because there's no such thing as situational integrity.

GOOD SAM

And since he was a partner in the agency, clients logically assumed that the other partners were of the same cut.

LANDOWNER

Because ungreat minds think alike. Hey, that could be that agency's motto! After all, would you trust something as important as your company's confidential marketing and advertising to a firm that not only lied about a dinky little project like the slide, but also ridiculed the client behind his back?

GOOD SAM

No, I wouldn't, and evidently neither would a lot of other people, because eventually several important clients left the agency, taking over $3 million in annual billings with them. The agency then had to fire employees as the partners scrambled to cut costs and stay afloat.

LANDOWNER

But you said the agency lost $60 million in billings. How?

GOOD SAM

They didn't just lose those clients for a single year, they lost them forever. And because of the agency's tarnished reputation, they also lost the friends and associates of those clients. Doors that might otherwise have been open became closed. Over 20 years the $60 million figure is probably low. It might top $100 million, if they manage to stay in business that long.

LANDOWNER

All because of a lazy no-talent dodo and his lunkhead buddies.

GOOD SAM

You know, I meant to say something about this earlier. I appreciate your sentiment, but I don't think we should stoop to name calling anymore. Okay? It's undignified.

LANDOWNER

You mean I shouldn't call those agency guys gutless little weenies who gained the trust of clients and then bilked them in order to hide their own breathtaking incompetence?

GOOD SAM

Correct. Now my second story happened when a billboard manager discussed campaign dates with his posting crew. The men complained that they often couldn't get the billboards up in time to meet the company's contractual promises.

LANDOWNER

Did the manager hire more workers?

GOOD SAM

No. He just told them it didn't matter if the clients got their full showings or not. His exact quote, said with an indifferent shrug, was "Who's going to know?"

LANDOWNER

When did he say that?

GOOD SAM

During a weekly staff meeting, in front of almost everyone in the branch.

LANDOWNER

So if clients lost a few thousand dollars of advertising time on their billboards, but didn't notice it, everything was all right. According to him.

GOOD SAM

Yes. And those two stories bring me to my point. The individuals discussed here do not belong in advertising. They've forgotten, if they ever knew, what a privilege it is to work with clients and help them accomplish their goals. It's an absolute kick to talk with a client, create a campaign, execute that campaign, and hear cash registers ring because of something that didn't even exist a few weeks earlier.

LANDOWNER

Creating something positive where nothing existed before. You make it sound like magic.

GOOD SAM

Properly done, advertising is magic. It's also fun, exciting, and rewarding. I can't imagine a better field to be in. But someone who abuses the trust of a client has lost his way, and the landowners should remember that when they take over the billboard industry. Nothing matters more than the clients. Nothing. Not what kind of sports car you drive, or how big your office is, or how many awards hang on your wall.

LANDOWNER

We should always focus on the clients.

GOOD SAM

Always. And be passionate. Make your moms proud of you. If you do, the money will come. You'll also sleep better at night, and you won't lose $60 million in billings.

LANDOWNER

I agree with you. I really do. But doesn't everyone say what you just said? Doesn't everyone say the client is important? In fact, didn't the people in these two stories claim to be client-focused?

GOOD SAM

You're right. They did. They faked it, but they faked it well.

LANDOWNER

So what do we do?

GOOD SAM

Work with people who don't fake it.

LANDOWNER

You make it sound easy.

GOOD SAM

Personnel selection is never easy. But it's essential. That's why the management team you eventually work with will be so important to your success.

LANDOWNER

One more question. Make our moms proud of us?

GOOD SAM

Hey, a business philosophy doesn't have to be complicated. If you need a star to steer by, that's one of the best you'll find.

Chapter 31

LANDOWNER

What's that piece of paper in your hand?

GOOD SAM

It's a fictional memo from a fictional billboard company owner to his fictional president. It's about our fictional conversation. Would you, as a fictional character, like to read it?

LANDOWNER

I'd love to.

GOOD SAM

Here you go.

TO: My Honorable Billboard Company President
FROM: Your Humble Company Owner
RE: Billboards

I've just read a wonderful and insightful book that I want distributed, at our expense, to all our landowners. It's a marvelous concept that encourages landowners to work together and explore business options that may or may not include their current billboard companies. Like all great works of literature, it takes complex subjects and makes them easy to understand.

The first thing you'll notice is that the book isn't relevant to our company. We already have open financial records for our beloved landowners, and we already pay a high percentage of total revenue. And if we eventually sell the company, our contracts already state that the landowners will receive a high percentage of the windfall.

But much to my dismay, I discovered that not all billboard companies are structured like ours. As crazy as it sounds, it appears some billboard companies don't appreciate the landowners the way we do. They don't recognize that without them we wouldn't have any company at all. Some even (and this is going to shock you) treat the landowners with disdain. But as they sowed, so shall they reap. Or, as you younger folk say: what goes around, comes around.

Chapter 32

LANDOWNER

Say, I don't know if you noticed, but I have a memo, too.

GOOD SAM

You have a memo? Jeepers, what a coincidence.

LANDOWNER

Isn't it? I mean, what are the odds? Interestingly enough, it's also from a fictional billboard company owner to his fictional president. Would you, as a fictional character, like to read it?

GOOD SAM

I'd love to.

LANDOWNER

Here you go.

TO: My Lackey Billboard Company President
FROM: Your Mighty and Exalted Leader
RE: Billboards

Listen up, you toady little wimp. We're cooked. Done. Finished. You know it, and I know it. The only thing left is to pull out as much money as possible before this sinking ship goes down.

Regarding our lenders and investors: Meet with them immediately. Lie to them them long enough for me to hide assets. Then shred everything. By the time they figure out they've been cheated, the money will be in offshore accounts and I'll be clear. If they come after us legally, we'll drag it out for decades and they'll never get a cent.

Regarding our *lessers*: They're nothing but cattle. But even dim-witted cows are dangerous in a stampede. So use your gift of gab to buy us some time. Twist things around. Muddy up the waters. Confuse them. They'll surely fall for it, because they always have, and they always will.

Regarding potential buyers: If some poor slob wants to buy this company, dump it on him. Fast. Falsify the numbers as we had always planned, then take him for whatever you can get. But keep him away from the landowners, or all my gleeful years of treachery and deceit will have been in vain.

Regarding our employees: Tell them to keep doing their stupid little jobs and living their stupid little lives as if nothing has happened. Then see how much we can steal from their 401-k funds.

Finally, make sure no one has copies of internal client or landowner lists. Those files have names, addresses, and phone numbers, and it would be devastating if they ever became public. I also don't want any copies of our All Branches financial statements getting out, because they include sales and profit figures for each individual market. In fact, I want everything to remain secret. Do you hear me? No talking. No blabbing. Secret!

When you're done, go take out the garbage at my $15 million vacation house. You missed some last week.

GOOD SAM

My goodness, what an, uh, interesting memo which is clearly not intended to reflect on any real people or companies, but is instead for entertainment purposes only.

Chapter 33

GOOD SAM

Well, that's it. We have to say good-bye. Maybe we'll meet again, maybe we won't. Should you be fortunate enough to someday find yourself in power, remember to treat your employees, and your clients, with the respect and honesty they deserve. Do that, and you'll achieve amazing things. In any case, I wish you the best.

LANDOWNER

Wait. We're done? I feel like there's more I should know.

GOOD SAM

There is more you should know. A lot more. For example, governmental Just Compensation payouts involve hundred of millions of dollars, yet you've probably never heard of them. Then there's insurance, anti-billboard legislation, corporate structure, and dozens of other important areas we haven't touched. But all that can be covered later. If you've paid attention, you know exactly what you and your fellow landowners have to do to start.

LANDOWNER

Call newspapers. Call bookstores. Visit courthouses to get landowner lists. Send everyone to the Web site.

GOOD SAM

Very good. Maybe you were listening after all.

LANDOWNER

But we better do these things fast, because enemies may already be plotting against us.

GOOD SAM

Yes. In the past, they mocked you. Sneered at you. Laughed behind your back. Now, they'll count on your apathy, indifference, and laziness. It's up to you to prove them wrong.

LANDOWNER

Or prove them right, as the case may be. If the landowners are weak, all the exciting things we've discussed will be impossible. If we don't care, no one else will care.

GOOD SAM

Say that again, please.

LANDOWNER

If we don't care, no one else will care.

GOOD SAM

That is exactly right. But if you do care, and you do take action, everyone else will follow your lead. Money, power, and the ability to do great good will be within your grasp, including the chance to perform true public service, and to positively influence nearly every community in the country.

LANDOWNER

Positively influence our communities. Can we sponsor kids' soccer teams?

GOOD SAM

You can do anything you want. You can even host charity golf tournaments, with celebrities and everything.

LANDOWNER

How will we learn about the tournaments?

GOOD SAM

From your monthly billboard landowner magazine.

LANDOWNER

And how will we subscribe to that?

GOOD SAM

Eventually, through the Web site. There will also be forms at your annual regional conventions, which will be held throughout the country by your national billboard landowner association.

LANDOWNER

That sounds fun. What will we wear?

GOOD SAM

Casual attire emblazoned with corporate logos.

LANDOWNER

I've never had clothes emblazoned with anything, let alone a corporate logo. This could be so neat.

GOOD SAM

It really could be. But it starts with you, and it starts now. You must create forward momentum. Don't rely on someone else to do it for you. In many markets, the actions of just one person will be the difference between success and failure.

LANDOWNER

Maybe you could help us by -

GOOD SAM

No. To the best of my ability, and in the time available to me, I've tried to educate you, entertain you, and motivate you. I can't do anything more without a strong show of interest from the landowners.

LANDOWNER

We have to prove we're deserving. The opportunity is in front of us, but it's not reality yet.

GOOD SAM

Correct. You must take action. Not next month. Not next week. Today, before it's too late. As you said earlier, billboard companies will likely have read this book. That means the secret is out, and the battle has begun. Tens of billions of dollars hang in the balance. The future is yours if you're strong enough to take it.

Read this last

When I was in college, I wrote a paper for a high level psychology class. It was the first paper of the semester, and it counted for a third of my final grade. To prepare, I read other psychology papers to get a sense of what was expected. Copying those styles, I used weighty words, sonorous sentences, and tumescent terminology. If it were any more stilted it could have worked in a circus. Sure enough, I got an A, and the professor noted how strong and persuasive it all was.

What a joke. I knew nothing about my topic, and had merely hidden my considerable ignorance behind a veil of quintessential quodlibetic gobbledygook. In hindsight, I don't think he even read the paper, which means he just glanced at it, decided it looked right, and went on to the next one.

Later, a second major paper was due for the same class. This time, I said to myself, I'm going to nail it. I studied, and studied, and studied. I knew my subject inside out and backwards. I discussed the topic with graduate students, and more than held my own. I mean, I really knew it. So I used simple language in the paper. Small words. Short sentences. Sometimes even fragments.

My goals were clarity and communication, nothing more. I was so proud of my work. So excited. So enthused. I got a B-. The professor said the paper lacked authoritative weight.

Such, sometimes, is life.

I tell you this because, as much as I try to ignore them, I hear the future cries of the critics. This odd little book about billboards is too long, they'll sniff. Or too short. Or it's too technical. Or not technical enough. But what they'll mean is it doesn't look like a business book. Deep down, they'll miss the security and familiarity of text more within their comfort zones. They'll miss the authoritative weight. And they might be right.

But a safer and more conservative approach may not have been any better, and may well have been a whole lot worse. Besides, my way was more fun, and despite my experience with the psych prof, I trust the reader to know the difference between style and substance. If some claim this material has neither style nor substance, well, I empathize with you. I repeatedly wrote things such as "united group" that surely made purists wince, and many fine rules of punctuation were probably neglected. But jeepers, what do you want, Haiku?

> Endless billboards stand
> watch in the cool quiet dawn
> change is coming soon

At least nothing was completely decimated, or returned from whence it came. Anyway, here it is, I did my best, and it will have to do, goofs and all. Letters of support will be appreciated. And if you have any interesting stories of your own regarding outdoor advertising, feel free to pass those along, too (especially if you are a landowner, or have been a client or employee of a billboard company).

* * *

Here's a recap:

1. Call newspapers and bookstores. Be nice.
2. Locate other landowners via government records.
3. Contact railroads first. They're the biggest.
4. Stay alert. Be wary of industry countermoves.
5. Talk with other landowners as much as you want.
6. Get offers from professional management teams.
7. Make informed, united decisions.
8. Sponsor kids' soccer teams. It'll be fun.
9. Be nice to trees and birds. They're living things, too.

* * *

Good luck to you all. Now go pick up the phone and call somebody.

Printed in the United States
1959